Class Structure and Economic Growth

Class Structure and Economic Growth

India and Pakistan since the Moghuls

by ANGUS MADDISON

W · W · NORTON & COMPANY · INC ·

NEW YORK

COPYRIGHT © 1971 BY GEORGE ALLEN & UNWIN LTD.

Library of Congress Catalog Card No. 79-37143

SBN 393 05467 5 (Cloth Edition)
SBN 393 09399 9 (Paper Edition)

This edition may not be sold outside the
United States of America, its dependencies, and
The Philippine Republic

PRINTED IN THE UNITED STATES OF AMERICA

1 2 3 4 5 6 7 8 9 0

Contents

Acknowledgements

I am grateful for criticism of earlier drafts which I received from Walter Falcon, Morton Grossman, Edward Kieloch, Millard Long, Edward S. Mason, Gustav Papanek, Tom Weisskopf; and to Sir Arthur Lewis for criticism of a very early draft of the historical chapters. I would like to thank Professor P. N. Dhar for early stimulus and hospitality in Delhi, and S. Sivasubramonian for allowing me to consult his unpublished manuscript on the national income of India.

I am grateful to Luigi Ceriani for allowing me to reproduce some of the material which I originally published in the *Quarterly Review* of the Banca Nazionale del Lavoro.

I received helpful comments from Professor Gerschenkron's seminar in economic history at Harvard and also from a seminar at the Center for International Affairs.

This book was written whilst I was a Research Fellow of the Center for International Affairs at Harvard University.

Tables

Chapter 1
Introduction

The purpose of this study is to analyse the relationship between social structure and economic performance in India and Pakistan. It seeks to establish whether the social system had a significant dysfunctional role in hindering growth in the past, and whether the situation has changed since independence. It analyses the extent to which governments in office really tried to change the social structure and the degree to which their rhetorical commitments were constrained by the inertia of tradition and by the vested interests which inherited economic and social power. It is interesting to compare India and Pakistan because they had a common history before 1947 and have since followed social policies which, in theory, are quite different. India has aimed to establish a 'socialist pattern' and to ensure that the benefits of growth filter down, whereas Pakistan in the 1960s proclaimed the need for functional inequality because of the alleged conflict between equity and growth.

Unfortunately, information on income distribution is poor and the social structure has such complex repercussions on growth that rigorous conclusions are not possible. However, it is hoped that the historical approach adopted here has at least the virtue of putting contemporary problems in perspective. The social structure of India and Pakistan is more complex than that of most countries, and survivals from the past have been tenacious. The present situation is a palimpsest impossible to decipher without historical analysis.

In the past two decades, the goal of economic growth has achieved the status of a secular religion. Economists have provided models explaining why and how it occurs, and governments have attempted to implement policies which ensure that it happens. These efforts have had some success. Both countries have had a modest but undeniable growth in real income per head after centuries of stagnation. Unfortunately, the material benefits of economic progress have not filtered down to the bottom half of the population. The degree of inequality has widened since independence. The overall effect of government action has been regressive in both countries. The tax system has had a negligible effect on income distribution, government expenditure has had a regressive impact, bureaucratic controls have favoured the rich, and land reforms and village uplift have done nothing for the bottom half of the rural population.

There is no evidence that the present distribution of income is particularly favourable for economic growth. The highly unequal distribution of land and the virtually complete tax exemption of the upper income groups in agriculture were an inheritance from the past which could not be changed without some temporary disturbance of production, but in the long run a more equitable system should make more productive use of land and labour. In industry, the policies of bureaucratic control which have promoted concentration of wealth and income have reduced efficiency in both countries. Greater use of market mechanisms and incentives in industry could have done more for both growth and equity. There are cases where the pursuit of equity might have reduced growth in the short run, e.g. a more determined effort to reduce disparity in income between East and West Pakistan, but postponement of such issues usually makes them more difficult to solve, and may reduce growth in the longer run.

Our conclusions about social development in the past two decades are therefore rather gloomy. The benefits of growth have accrued largely to the upper income groups, the inequities have no functional justification, and growth has been below potential. However, this is not a new phenomenon in India and Pakistan, as is clear from Chapter II on the Moghul economy and Chapter III on the colonial period.

In many respects the Moghul economy was highly sophisticated and its performance at times matched that of Western Europe, but the social structure involved a high degree of exploitation through fiscal and caste mechanisms. The fiscal system with its heavy reliance on land tax had some analogy with that of Manchu China and Tokugawa Japan, but caste was unique. Both the fiscal system and caste had dysfunctional elements. At its best, under Akbar, the fiscal system worked reasonably well, but the primary economic aim of the Moghul elite was short-term maximization of the tax levy on the villages. It was a regime of warlords and not a bureaucracy. By squeezing too hard, the Moghul elite reduced productivity and inhibited capital formation. The caste hierarchy within village society also lowered productivity by (a) pushing the living standards of the lowest groups down to a level which reduced physical working capacity and eliminated incentives for increased output, (b) allocating jobs on a rigid basis of heredity rather than aptitude, (c) instilling a ritualistic rather than functional attitude to work, (d) maintaining taboos on the use of animal husbandry and manure which kept productivity low. The Moghul superstructure has now disappeared, but village society, the bureaucracy, and some parts of the urban economy are still permeated by the same type of ritual inequality which is harmful to economic efficiency.

Colonial rule had important consequences. The social pyramid was truncated at the top. The claim of the Moghul aristocracy on national income went down from 15 per cent to the 3 per cent made available to those princes and *zamindars* kept on by the British. Their decline ruined the market for the Indian handicraft industry. Part of the Moghul surplus was transferred to the upper-caste village capitalists and money-lenders, thus increasing income inequality within the villages. Part of the fiscal resources previously used to support the Moghuls was used to create a modern military-bureaucratic machine. The modernizing activities of the new bureaucratic elite were sufficient to stimulate growth in population and output, but not to increase *per capita* income. A modern industrial and commercial sector was created on a limited scale with a heavy dependence on British managing agencies and very limited diffusion of modern skills to Indians. If India had not been subjected to colonial rule its history would probably have been like that of China. Its population would have been smaller because of internal wars and political divisions, but there would have been a bigger economic surplus available for a late-coming group of modern-izers.

Chapter IV provides a brief résumé of the ideological background of the nationalist movements in India and Pakistan. Chapter V analyses the major factors which have led to an acceleration of economic growth since independence. Both of these important subjects are treated in somewhat brusque and summary fashion, but I hope these chapters may be useful in providing a background to the main discussion of social structure since independence, which is contained in Chapters VI and VII.

Since independence, the major changes in social structure in India and Pakistan have been the transformation of the Moghul remnants (zamindars and princes) into state pensioners, a reduction in the role of foreign capitalists, a growth in the local capitalist and professional classes, a sharp expansion of the size of the military-bureaucratic group, and a further widening of income differentials in the country-side. Growth has been faster because the bureaucracy has been able to act as a modernizing elite, on similar lines to those in Meiji Japan (but with more reliance on inefficient protective devices to foster industrialization), and village capitalists have played a more productive role than they did in the colonial period. The pattern is basically similar in India and Pakistan, in spite of the apparently fundamental differences in social policy.

The social structure has not experienced radical change. A key element of stability has been the bureaucratic elite which is at least as important as in colonial times, jealously guarding its perquisites and imposing a clientistic status on industrial capitalists through a network of direct controls. Similarly, the village capitalists cling to their caste privileges, land rights and freedom from taxation. Indian social policy since independence has placed considerable emphasis on the natural harmony of interest within the village 'community'. In fact, the village is not a community; it is simply the locus of production in the agrarian sector. There is no more harmony in the village 'community' than there is in the urban 'community'. Within the village there is a fourfold hierarchy of rural capitalists, working proprietors, sharecropping tenants and landless labourers. Their interests are not harmonious but conflicting.

In both India and Pakistan, the social structure is now showing considerable strain, and changes may well be in the offing. However, there are so many conservative elements at the top, and the poor are so weak, unorganized and debilitated that changes are likely to be reformist and piecemeal rather than fundamental. The probability in both countries is that government slogans will be increasingly populist, that real reform will be extremely slow, and that economic growth will be below potential.

It is not difficult to prescribe policies which might have done or might do more to promote equity and growth. Some of these are adumbrated here. However, most of the theoretical options are foreclosed by pressure of vested interests, even when sanctioned by legislation. It is misleading to treat the bureaucratic apparatus as a neutral instrument which can be bent to any kind of policy. The bureaucracy itself is a complex social structure and a powerful vested interest, as we have gone to some pains to demonstrate. There is no point in writing blueprints for social change, unless the bureaucracy itself is reformed.

Chapter II
The Moghul Economy and Society

The pre-colonial economy of India is sometimes portrayed by Indian historians and politicians as a golden age of prosperity. According to R. C. Dutt, the doyen of nationalist historians, 'India in the eighteenth century was a great manufacturing as well as a great agricultural country'.[1] Gandhi and others have stressed the social harmony of the traditional village society. These views have been very influential and it is obviously important to see whether they stand up to critical analysis. Our own conclusion is that they exaggerate the productivity of the Moghul economy which was probably significantly lower than that of west Europe in the eighteenth century.

The Standard of Living

India had a ruling class whose extravagant life-style surpassed that of the European aristocracy. It had an industrial sector producing luxury goods which Europe could not match, but this was achieved by subjecting the population to a high degree of exploitation. Living standards of ordinary people were lower than those of European peasants and their life expectation was shorter. The high degree of exploitation was possible because of the passivity of village society. The social mechanism which kept the villages passive also lowered labour productivity, and provided little incentive to technical progress or productive investment.

Moghul India had a good deal to impress Western visitors. From the time of Akbar to Shah Jehan the court was one of the most brilliant in the world. It was cosmopolitan and religiously tolerant. Literature and painting flourished and there were magnificent palaces and mosques at Agra, Delhi, Fatehpur Sikri, and Lahore. The nobility lived in walled castles with harems, gardens, fountains and large retinues of slaves and servants. They had huge wardrobes of splendid garments in fine cotton and silk.

In order to cater for their needs, a number of handicraft industries produced high quality cotton textiles, silks, jewellery, decorative swords and weapons. These luxury industries grew up in urban

[1] See R. C. Dutt, *The Economic History of India 1757–1837*, Government of India reprint, Delhi, 1963, p. xxv.

centres. The urban population was bigger in the Muslim period than it had been under Hindu rulers, for caste restrictions had previously kept artisans out of towns.[1] Most urban workers were Muslims.[2] The main market for these urban products was domestic, but a significant portion of luxury textiles was exported either to Europe or South-East Asia. Other export items were saltpetre (for gunpowder), indigo, sugar, opium and ginger. Europeans had great difficulty in finding products to exchange for these Indian luxuries. They were able to export a few woollen goods and some metals, but the only things the Indians really wanted in exchange and which were worth the cost of transporting so far were precious metals.[3] There was, therefore, a constant flow of silver and gold to India, which absorbed a good deal of the bullion produced by the Spaniards in the New World. It was this phenomenon which most impressed and disturbed Europeans in their relations with India.

According to the testimony of European travellers, some of the urban centres of Moghul India were bigger than the biggest cities in Europe at the same period.[4] We do not know whether the overall

---

[1] See B. N. Ganguli (ed.), *Readings in Indian Economic History*, Asia Publishing House, London, 1964, p. 55.

[2] See I. H. Qureshi, *The Muslim Community of the Indo-Pakistan Sub-Continent* (610–1947), Mouton, The Hague, 1962, p. 219: 'The courts had been great consumers of the various articles produced by Muslim craftsmen. All the finer qualities of textiles like Dacca muslin and Kashmir shawls were woven by Muslim master weavers. The manufacture of rich carpets was a Muslim monopoly. The rich brocades which had been in fashion both among men and women of means were made by Muslims. The manufacture of the more delicately finished jewellery, inlay work in silver and gold, and the creation of many articles of beauty so highly prized by the wealthy classes were almost entirely in Muslim hands.'

[3] The same was true in China whose emperor wrote to George III: 'The Celestial Empire possesses all things in prolific abundance and lacks no product within its borders. There is therefore no need to import the manufactures of outside barbarians in exchange for our own products.' See E. Backhouse and J. O. P. Bland, *Annals and Memoirs of the Court of Peking*, 1914, p. 326.

[4] For example, Clive considered that Murshidabad was more prosperous than London—see J. Nehru, *Glimpses of World History*, Lindsay Drummond, London, 1945, p. 417: 'Clive has described the city of Murshidabad in Bengal in 1757, as a city as extensive, populous, and rich as the city of London, with this difference, that there are individuals in the first possessing infinitely greater property than in the last.' Nehru does not give the source of this quotation from Clive which is also cited by R. Palme Dutt, and I have not been able to trace the original source. Bernier had a poorer view of Indian cities: 'It is because of these wretched clay and straw houses that I always represent Delhi as a collection of many villages, or as a military encampment with a few more conveniences than are usually found in such places.' See F. Bernier, *Travels in the Moghul Empire*, London, 1826, Vol. I, p. 281. I. Habib suggests that Agra was the biggest seventeenth-

ratio of urban to total population was bigger or smaller than in Europe,[1] but the climate made it possible to get double and treble cropping in some areas, so it was technically possible (with a given transport system) to support bigger towns than in Europe. Most of the luxury handicraft trades were located in cities, and there was also a well-established banking system for the transfer of funds from one part of India to another. In urban society, occupation was controlled by guild regulation and a hereditary caste structure, but occupational mobility was greater than in villages because town life was dominated by Muslims, or, in some commercial areas, by Europeans.

European traders dominated the export business from the sixteenth century onwards. Before that, India had traded in textile products with East Africa, the Persian Gulf, Malaya and Indonesia. The Europeans opened up new markets in Europe, West Africa and the Philippines, and their trading companies built up production centres for textiles, indigo and saltpetre in Gujarat, Coromandel and Bengal. They introduced new techniques of dyeing and silk-winding and set up large-scale factory production for the first time. On the whole, European activity increased the productivity of the Indian economy,[2] though at times Europeans did extort monopoly profits, i.e. in the first phase of Portuguese monopoly (sixteenth century), and in the thirty years after the East India Company conquered Bengal. One of the reasons foreigners dominated this trade was that religious beliefs inhibited foreign travel and commercial development by Hindus. The export trade was in the hands of Arabs, Armenians and Jews until Europeans established trading settlements in the coastal towns.

The luxury of court life, the international trade in silks and muslins, the large size and splendour of some Indian cities, the disdain for European products—these were the reasons why Moghul India was

---

century town with a population of 500,000 to 600,000. See I. Habib, *The Agrarian System of Moghul India, 1556–1707*, Asia Publishing House, London, 1963, p. 76.

[1] There are no statistics on the size of urban population before the 1872 census when it was 10 per cent of total population. Professor Gadgil suggests that the proportion was probably about the same at the beginning of British rule. See D. R. Gadgil, *The Industrial Evolution of India in Modern Times*, Oxford University Press, 1950, p. 6.

[2] See T. Raychaudhuri, 'European Commercial Activity and the Organization of India's Commerce and Industrial Production 1500–1750', in B. N. Ganguli (ed.), *op. cit.*, pp. 75–6: 'To sum up, the impact of European commerce with India on a competitive basis was in many ways beneficient. New markets were opened for Indian exports and the existing ones further deepened. For the limited areas supplying the staples of export, this meant an increase in production and probably also in productivity.'

regarded as wealthy by some European travellers. The living standard of the upper class was certainly high and there were bigger hoards of gold and precious stones than in Europe, but there is substantial evidence that the mass of the population were worse off than in Europe. The Moghul economy seems to have been at its peak under Akbar (1556–1605) and to have declined thereafter.[1] At its peak, it is conceivable that the *per capita* product was comparable with that of Elizabethan England. By the mid eighteenth century, when India became a European colony, there seems little doubt that the economy was backward by West European standards, with a *per capita* product perhaps two-thirds of that in England and France.[2]

In spite of India's reputation as a cloth producer, Abul Fazl, the sixteenth-century chronicler of Akbar, makes reference to the lack of clothing in Bengal, 'men and women for the most part go naked wearing only a cloth about the loins'. Their loincloths were often of jute rather than cotton. In Orissa 'the women cover only the lower part of the body and may make themselves coverings of the leaves of trees'.[3] They also lacked the domestic linen and blankets, which European peasants of that period would have owned. In terms of housing and furniture the Indian peasantry were worse off than their European counterparts and their diet was also poorer. Consumption of meat and wine was negligible and there was no beer.

Conditions in the early seventeenth century were described by Francisco Pelsaert in a report to the Dutch East India Company which sums up his seven years in Agra in 1620–7:

'. . . the rich in their great superfluity and absolute power, and the utter subjection and poverty of the common people—poverty so

[1] See W. H. Moreland, *India at the Death of Akbar*, A. Ram, Delhi, 1962, for a description of living conditions at the end of the sixteenth century. Moreland suggests that the degree of exploitation increased under Jehangir and Shah Jehan, and that this had adverse effects both on economic efficiency and popular living standards. See W. H. Moreland, *From Akbar to Aurangzeb*, Macmillan, London, 1923.

[2] See A. Maddison, 'Comparative Productivity Levels in the Developed Countries', *Banca Nazionale del Lavoro Quarterly Review*, December 1967, which gives figures of income levels for France and England in the eighteenth century (about $250 at 1965 U.S. prices around mid-century). India's *per capita* income in 1750 was probably similar to that in 1950, i.e. about $150 at 1965 U.S. prices (see A. Maddison, *Economic Progress and Policy in Developing Countries*, Norton, New York, 1970, p. 18). For an extrapolation of Indian income back to the Moghul period, see T. Raychaudhuri, 'A Reinterpretation of Nineteenth Century Indian Economic History', *Indian Economic and Social History Review*, March 1968, p. 90.

[3] See H. S. Jarett and J. Sarkar (eds), *Ain-I-Akbari of Abul Fazl-I-Allami*, Vol. II, Calcutta, 1949, pp. 134 and 138.

great and miserable that the life of the people can be depicted or accurately described only as the home of stark want and the dwelling place of bitter woe . . . a workman's children can follow no occupation other than that of their father, nor can they inter-marry with any other caste. . . . They know little of the taste of meat. For their monotonous daily food they have nothing but a little *khichri*, made of "green pulse" mixed with rice, which is cooked with water over a little fire until the moisture has evapor-ated, and eaten hot with butter in the evening; in the day time they munch a little parched pulse or other grain, which they say suffices for their lean stomachs.

'Their houses are built of mud with thatched roofs. Furniture there is little or none . . . bedclothes are scanty, merely a sheet or perhaps two, serving both as under- and over-sheet; this is sufficient in the hot weather, but the bitter cold nights are miserable indeed.'[1]

The domestic market for Indian silks and muslins was concentrated on the upper class, and the export market was not very large in relation to the economy as a whole. In 1780, before Indian textiles were hit by competition from the industrial revolution, exports from Bengal were less than £2 million—much smaller than those of the U.K., which had less than a tenth of its population.[2]

Although the man–land ratio was similar to that in France or England, agricultural output per head was almost certainly lower in India in the eighteenth century.[3] It also seems likely that productivity was lower than in China or Japan.[4] Fairly large areas were devoted

[1] See the translation by W. H. Moreland and P. Geyl, *Jahangir's India*, Heffer, Cambridge, 1925, pp. 60–1.

[2] British exports in 1780 were £12·6 million (including re-exports of £4·6 million). See B. R. Mitchell and P. Deane, *Abstract of British Historical Statistics*, Cambridge University Press, 1962, p. 280. For the exports of Bengal, see N. K. Sinha, *The Economic History of Bengal*, Mukopadhyay, Calcutta, 1961.

[3] For a description of Indian agriculture in the Moghul period, see I. Habib, *op. cit.* For Europe, see B. H. Slicher van Bath, *The Agrarian History of Western Europe A.D. 500–1850*, Arnold, London, 1963.

[4] A. Eckstein, *The National Income of Communist China*, Free Press, Glencoe, 1961, p. 67, shows Chinese crop output per head 29 per cent above that in India, livestock output 9 per cent lower and total agricultural output per head 22 per cent higher than in India (at Indian prices) in 1952. As China had passed through a century of severe disturbance, it seems likely that its relative advantage was even bigger in the eighteenth century. For Japan, see T. C. Smith, *The Agrarian Origins of Modern Japan*, Oxford University Press, 1959. According to S. Ishikawa, *Conditions for Agricultural Development in Developing Asian Countries*, Committee for Translation of Japanese Economic Studies, Tokyo, the rice yield in Japan was 2·4 tons per hectare in the seventeenth century and 2·3 tons per

to low-quality grains like *bajra* or *jowar*—the unreliable weather was one of the reasons for growing these, for they were more resistant to weather fluctuations than wheat or rice. Farm implements were poor and ploughs were made of wood. Crop residues were not used for compost as in China,[1] and cow dung was used as a fuel or building material rather than for manure. Human excrement was considered defiling to caste Hindus and not used, nor were bone meal or oil seeds used as in China or Japan. Crops were damaged by rodent and insect pests which were not checked for religious reasons. Indian agriculture did not benefit as much as Europe and Africa from the new American crops available from the sixteenth century onwards. Potatoes, maize and cassava remained unimportant, and tobacco was the only significant novelty. The irrigated area was small.

There were more cattle than in Europe, but milk yields were much lower.[2] The brahmins and a large part of the rest of the population were vegetarians, and meat consumption was very low. Cattle were used for traction in agriculture, horses were a luxury.

Life expectation was lower than in Europe, but fertility was higher because marriage was obligatory for social and religious reasons, and virtually all girls were married before puberty.[3] Death rates were higher for several reasons. Reliance on the monsoon meant that agricultural output fluctuated more than in Europe, and famine was therefore more frequent. Health conditions were worse, partly because of poor diet, partly for other reasons. The climate was debilitating. There were tropical diseases as well as the European ones. Hindu taboos against killing rodents and insects led to longer persistence of bubonic plague. Hindu distaste for touching refuse or excreta led to greater squalor and lack of sanitation. Infanticide of

---

hectare in China as early as the tenth century. In India it was only half of this in the 1950s.

[1] See A. Howard and G. L. C. Howard, *The Development of Indian Agriculture*, Oxford University Press, London, 1929, p. 49.

[2] But I. Habib, *op. cit.*, p. 53 makes the point that there was probably more pasturage, more cattle, manure, milk and ghi per head in the seventeenth century than there is now. For European milk yields from the sixteenth century onwards, see B. H. Slicher van Bath, *op. cit.*, p. 335.

[3] See T. Raychaudhuri, *Bengal under Akbar and Jehangir*, Mukherjee, Calcutta, 1953, p. 186. 'For girls, seven was considered to be the ideal age for marriage and the age-limit of twelve could be crossed only at the cost of grave social opprobrium.' In Europe, before the fifteenth century, girls usually married at puberty, but by the seventeenth century the general European pattern was one of late marriage, the average age for women being twenty-four, see J. Hajnal, 'European Marriage Patterns in Perspective', in D. V. Glass and D. E. C. Eversley, *Population in History*, Arnold, London, 1965.

daughters[1] and 'suicide' of widows added substantially to mortality in some areas. Finally, maternal and child mortality was high because girls started to become mothers at the age of twelve. Their inexperience and physical immaturity led to high death rates.[2] Kingsley Davis has suggested that mortality rates in India were high enough to offset the very high fertility rates, so that there was little increase in population in the 2,000 years preceding European rule.[3]

Education facilities and the content of education were no better than in medieval Europe, and much worse than in Europe after the Renaissance. Muslim education was entirely religious and carried out in *madrassas* where boys learned the Koran in Arabic. Although the Moghul period was distinguished for its architecture, painting, poetry and music, these were largely derived from foreign models, particularly those of Safavid Persia. Hindu education was confined to religious instruction for higher-caste boys in Sanscrit. Neither religious group provided education for women. It has been suggested that at the time of the British takeover about a quarter of the male population had received a few years of schooling, that most brahmins could read and write, and the literacy rate was about 5 per cent.[4] There was no Hindu higher education of a secular character. Earlier Indian Buddhist universities (e.g. Nalanda) had been destroyed by the Muslim invaders. The theology of Hinduism did not encourage the growth of rational thought, and the social system hindered technical innovation. In spite of extensive contact with foreigners, India did not copy foreign technology either in shipping or navigation, or in artillery and military organization, and this is one of the reasons it was conquered by Europeans.

[1] See M. Weber, *The Religion of India*, Free Press, Glencoe, 1958, p. 42: 'Despite the severe English laws of 1829, as late as 1869, in twenty-two villages of Rajputana there were 23 girls and 284 boys. In an 1836 count, in the same Rajput area, not one single live girl of over one year of age was found in a population of 10,000!'

[2] See K. Mayo, *Mother India*, Harcourt Brace, New York, 1927, for a description of the impact of child marriage on the physical and mental health of women.

[3] See K. Davis, *The Population of India and Pakistan*, Princeton University Press, 1951, p. 24. In China by contrast there was a threefold increase in population from 1393 to 1750 and a matching rise in agricultural output—see D. H. Perkins, *Agricultural Development in China 1368–1968*, Aldine, Chicago, 1969, p. 216. However, the evidence on Indian population is very slender. Davis's conclusion was based on interpolation between the estimates of Moreland and Pran Nath. Davis adjusted Moreland upwards by a quarter, and the basis for Nath's estimates is even more shaky. It is quite possible that population may have risen substantially in the 2,000 years preceding European rule.

[4] See S. Nurullah and J. P. Naik, *A History of Education in India*, Macmillan, Bombay, 1951. Teaching was done largely on a monitorial system, which was

The Degree of Exploitation

The revenue of the Moghul state was derived largely from land tax which was about a third or more of gross crop production (i.e. a quarter or more of total agricultural output including fruits, vegetables and livestock products which were not so heavily taxed).[1] Other levies, tolls and taxes were of smaller importance but not negligible. Total revenue of the Moghul state and autonomous princelings and chiefs was probably about 15–18 per cent of national income. By European standards of the same period this was a very large tax burden.[2] No European government succeeded in claiming such a large part of the national product until the twentieth century. But there was a fundamental difference in social structure between India and Europe, and the Moghul levy should not be compared with taxes in a European country. Taxes were used not only for state purposes but to provide for the consumption expenditure of the ruling class. They were, therefore, equal to the tax revenue and a large part of the rental income of a European country (not to the whole of rents because the upper layer within the village hierarchy retained some of the rental income).

In India the aristocracy were not hereditary landlords whose income was derived by using serfs to cultivate their private demesne. They did not possess land of their own, but were either paid in cash or allocated the tax revenue from a collection of villages (i.e. they were given a *jagir*).[3] Part of the revenue was for their own sustenance, the rest was to be paid to the central treasury in cash or in the form of troop support. The aristocracy was not, in principle, hereditary, and a considerable part of it consisted of foreigners. Moghul practice derived from the traditions of the nomadic societies which had created Islam in Arabia as well as similar Turkic traditions. Nobles were regularly posted from one jagir to another and their estates

---

copied in England in the first few decades of the nineteenth century where it was known as the Madras system.

[1] For Moghul taxation, see I. Habib, *op. cit.* There is no evidence that the burden of land tax was any lighter in areas under Hindu rule than in those controlled by the Moghuls. W. H. Moreland suggests that the revenue demand in the Hindu kingdom of Vijayanagar was bigger than in Moghul territories. See W. H. Moreland, *op. cit.* Mrs Boserup also quotes evidence that revenue demands in pre-Muslim times could be much higher than the sixth of gross agricultural product prescribed by the Hindu code (the laws of Manu). See E. Boserup, *The Conditions of Agricultural Growth*, Allen and Unwin, London, 1965, p. 98.

[2] In England, the tax revenue amounted to 6·3 per cent of national income in 1688. See P. Deane and W. A. Cole, *British Economic Growth 1688–1959*, Cambridge University Press, 1964, p. 2.

[3] For a description of the system, see M. A Ali, *The Moghul Nobility under Aurangzeb*, Asia Publishing House, London, 1966.

were liable to royal forfeit on death. This system led to a wasteful use of resources. There was little motive to improve landed property. The *jagirdar* had an incentive to squeeze village society close to subsistence, to spend as much as possible on consumption and to die in debt to the state. This was true at the apex of the system as well, because the succession to the throne, though theoretically hereditary, was in fact often a matter of very costly dispute. Apart from the jagirdars, there were some Hindu nobles (zamindars)[1] who retained hereditary control over village revenues, and Hindu princes who continued to rule and collect revenues in autonomous states within the Moghul Empire, e.g. in Rajputana. Towards the end of the Moghul period, as central power declined, many jagirs became hereditary in practice. But the ruling class always obtained its income by levying tribute on villages, it did not enter into the process of production.

It should be stressed that the uses to which the Moghul state and aristocracy put their income were largely unproductive. Their investments were made in two main forms: (*a*) hoarding precious metals and jewels (India's imports of precious metals were equal to practically the whole of its exports and there was also some internal production of these items); (*b*) construction of palaces and tombs, particularly under Shah Jehan.[2] There were also some public irrigation works but, in the context of the economy as a whole, these were unimportant and probably did not cover more than 5 per cent of the cultivated land of India. It is misleading in the Indian context to suggest, as Marx did, that the 'oriental despotism' of the state apparatus had a functional justification in the development and protection of irrigation.[3] As far as the economy was concerned the

---

[1] In Bengal, in the 1720s, under the Muslim subahdar, Murshid Quli, 'more than three-fourths of the zamindars, big and small, and most of the talukdars were Hindus'. N. K. Sinha, *op. cit.*, p. 4. This was the case in a province where the majority of the peasants were Muslims.

[2] See W. H. Moreland, *From Akbar to Aurangzeb*, Macmillan, London, 1923, pp. 195–7.

[3] Marx put forward the idea as a general characteristic of Asia: 'This prime necessity of an economical and common use of water, which in the Occident, drove private enterprise to voluntary association, as in Flanders and Italy, necessitated in the Orient where civilization was too low and the territorial extent too vast to call into life voluntary association, the interference of the centralizing power of Government. Hence an economical function devolved upon all Asiatic Governments, the function of providing public works.' See article in the *New York Daily Tribune*, June 25, 1853. The article is quoted in S. Avineri, *Karl Marx on Colonialism and Modernization*, Doubleday, New York, 1969. The theme of 'hydraulic' society is developed at length by K. A. Wittfogel, *Oriental Despotism*, Yale University Press, 1957. My estimate of a 5 per cent irrigation

Moghul state apparatus was parasitic. It therefore seems inappropriate to call the system an agrarian bureaucracy. It was a regime of warlord predators which was less efficient than European feudalism. Its adverse effects on output have been described vividly by Bernier.[1]

Moghul officials needed high incomes because they had many dependents to support. They maintained polygamous households with vast retinues of slaves and servants. Military spending was also large because there were so many soldiers, and they were frequently engaged in wars. Religion was probably just as big an economic burden as in Europe, but not in such a direct way. Religious property was smaller, with rather modest tax-free land grants and no hierarchically organized priesthood. But there was a vast band of religious mendicants to be supported and considerable expense in carrying out weddings and funerals in a way which satisfied religious scruples.

The Docility of Village Society

The reason why the Moghuls could raise so much revenue from taxation, without having a ruling class which directly supervised the production process, was that village society was very docile. This docility was not ensured by a church hierarchy, but by a subtle network of internal sanctions which existed nowhere else in the world.

The chief characteristic of Indian society which differentiated it from others was the institution of caste. The origins of caste are shrouded in antiquity. It segregates the population into mutually

---

ratio is a guess. In 1850 the ratio was about 3·5 per cent and only 7·5 million acres were irrigated—see *The First Five Year Plan*, Delhi, December 1952, p. 338. Even if the absolute size of the irrigated area was as big as this under the Moghuls, the proportion would not have been bigger than 5 per cent.

[1] Bernier was a well-connected seventeenth-century traveller, who lived in India for twelve years and was a physician to Aurangzeb. He says in a letter to Colbert: 'As the ground is seldom tilled otherwise than by compulsion, and as no person is found willing and able to repair the ditches and canals for the conveyance of water, it happens that the whole country is badly cultivated, and a great part rendered unproductive from the want of irrigation. The houses, too, are left in a dilapidated condition, there being few people who will either build new ones, or repair those which are tumbling down. The peasant cannot avoid asking himself this question: "Why should I toil for a tyrant who may come tomorrow and lay his rapacious hands upon all I possess and value, without leaving me, if such should be his humour, the means to drag on my miserable existence." The *timariots*, governors and farmers, on their part reason in this manner: "Why should the neglected state of this land create uneasiness in our minds? and why should we expend our own money and time to render it fruitful? we may be deprived of it in a single moment, and our exertions would benefit neither ourselves nor our children. Let us draw from the soil all the money we can, though the peasant should starve or abscond, and we should leave it, when commanded to quit, a dreary wilderness." ' See F. Bernier, *op. cit.*

exclusive groups whose economic and social functions are clearly defined and hereditary. Old religious texts classify Hindus into four main groups: *brahmins*, a caste of priests at the top of the social scale whose ceremonial purity was not to be polluted by manual labour; next in priority came the *kshatriyas* or warriors, thirdly the *vaishyas* or traders, and finally the *sudras*, or farmers. Below this there were *melechas* or outcastes to perform menial and unclean tasks.

But this old theoretical model of the Rigveda is somewhat misleading. In each main linguistic area of India there are about two hundred separate caste groups with their own name, and each of these is likely to be divided into about ten sub-castes which are the effective boundaries of social life.[1] Brahmins and untouchables are distinguishable everywhere, but the classification of intermediate castes is unclear and often does not conform to the kshatriya, vaishya, sudra categorization. In each village there will be a caste which is economically and socially dominant, and in many villages this dominant caste will be a peasant caste. In all parts of India there are outcastes at the bottom (they are now about 15 per cent of the population), and the presence of these 'untouchables' gives all caste Hindus a feeling of superior social status no matter how poor they may be themselves.

Members of different castes did not intermarry or eat together, and kept apart in social life. Their dress, names and housing were quite distinctive. 'Corresponding to the caste hierarchy are hierarchies in food, occupation and styles of life. The highest castes are vegetarians as well as teetotallers, while the lowest eat meat (including domestic pork and beef) and consume indigenous liquor. Consumption of the meat of such a village scavenger as the pig pollutes the eaters, while the ban on beef comes from the high place given to the cow in the sacred texts of Hinduism. Among occupations, those involving manual work are rated lower than those which do not.'[2]

The great variety of caste was due to the large size of the country and the ethnic and linguistic diversity which had developed over millenia of settlement. It was also due to the process by which Hinduism spread. Invaders or aboriginal tribes were assimilated gradually into the Hindu fold. They were not converted to a clearly defined religion or incorporated into an organized hierarchical structure. The system was too amorphous and permissive for that. New entrants could keep their own customs and gods. However,

---

[1] See G. S. Ghurye, *Caste, Class and Occupation*, Popular Book Depot, Bombay, 1961, pp. 26–7.

[2] See M. N. Srinivas, *Social Change in Modern India*, Berkeley, 1966, p. 120.

groups trying to improve their ritual status generally copied the behaviour patterns of the locally dominant caste. This mimicry of dominant caste characteristics has been called 'sanscritization' by India's leading sociologist Srinivas.[1] Thus brahminical habits in diet (vegetarianism and teetotalism), taboos on widow remarriage or divorce, the requirement that girls marry before puberty, grew more widespread over time. There was some mobility in the system for castes if not for individuals. Changes in ritual status were most easily attainable by castes which had improved their economic status, e.g. by political conquest, or by establishing a new village.[2]

In each village the dominant caste controlled the land, though their property rights were circumscribed. In general, land would not be transferred or sold to people outside the village, and tenants of the dominant caste could not be evicted. Most villagers belonged to cultivating castes, with each family tending customary but unequal shares of the land. Brahmins were not cultivators, but acted as a local priesthood or squirearchy in alliance with the locally dominant caste and used low caste or untouchable labourers to cultivate their land. In each village there were artisans who provided non-agricultural goods and services, e.g. blacksmiths, carpenters, potters, cobblers, weavers, washermen, barbers, water carriers, astrologers, watchmen and, occasionally, dancing girls. Spinning was not a specialized craft but was carried out by village women. These artisan families did not sell their products for money but had a hereditary patron–client (*jajmani*) relationship with a group of cultivating families. Thus a washerman or barber would serve a family's wants free throughout the year and get payment in kind at harvest time. In addition, there was a lower class of untouchable village servants to perform menial tasks, e.g. sweeping, removal of human and animal manure, in return for payment in kind.

In relations with the state, the village usually acted as a unit. In particular, land taxes were usually paid collectively and the internal allocation of the burden was left to the village headman or accountant. The village council (*panchayat*) ran the internal affairs of the village, provided a village policeman and settled disputes about land. Caste panchayats settled other social problems and disputes. In view of the heavy fiscal squeeze on the village from above, and the possibility

[1] See M. N. Srinivas, *Caste in Modern India*, Asia Publishing House, Bombay, 1962, Chapter 2.

[2] Other means of improving economic status became more frequent under British rule and the beginning of modern economic growth. See F. G. Bailey, *Caste and the Economic Frontier*, Manchester University Press, 1957, who gives examples of castes in Orissa whose economic status was changed by entrepreneurship as distillers, and who subsequently improved their caste status.

of quitting a village to farm surplus land which was generally available elsewhere, one would have expected the social structure within villages to be fairly egalitarian. Income differentials were probably smaller than they are now, but the village was not an idyllic commune as is sometimes claimed. In fact, the practice of describing the village as a 'community' is misleading because it implies a much greater degree of common interest than actually existed. Over most of the country there was a dominant caste elite, an intermediate group of cultivators and artisans and a bottom layer of landless untouchables, each group with differing levels of real income. These intra-village differentials varied geographically and changed over time according to the degree of outside fiscal pressure, but all over the country the top group in the village were allies of the state, co-beneficiaries in the system of exploitation.[1] In every village the bottom layer were untouchables squeezed tight against the margin of subsistence. The extra-village exploitation was sanctioned by military force, intra-village exploitation by the caste system and its religious sanctions. Without the caste sanctions, village society would probably have been more egalitarian, and a more homogeneous peasantry might have been less willing to put up with such heavy fiscal levies from the warlord state.

From an economic point of view, the most interesting feature of caste in traditional society is that it fixed a man's occupation by heredity. For priests or barbers the prospect of doing the same job as a whole chain of ancestors was perhaps not too depressing but for those whose hereditary function was to clean latrines, the system offered no joys in this world. One reason they accepted it was the general belief in reincarnation which held out the hope of rebirth in a higher social status to those who acquired merit by loyal performance of their allotted task in this world.

One problem in this system of formalized hereditary interdependence was that family needs or production capacity could change over time for demographic reasons. If barbers or washermen were particularly fertile over a couple of generations there would soon be too many of them. There was some flexibility in the system which permitted changing patron–client relationships, inter-village

[1] See B. B. Misra, *The Indian Middle Classes*, Oxford University Press, London, 1961, '. . . before the coming of the British, the influence which dominated a village community was that of a particular kin, especially the Brahmans and Rajputs, who owned most villages, either as village zamindars in the upper provinces and parts of Bihar or as *taluqdars* in Bengal; as *mirasdars* in the South or *inamdars* in the West. The other occupational groups worked in subservience to the dominant landed interest of a village. . . . Fundamentally the inferior occupational groups functioned more or less in bondage in all situations.'

mobility of labour, or even changes in occupation which did not do too much violence to caste rules.[1]

No modern trade union has been so jealous about job specification as the caste system. It did not merely prevent a man from increasing his productivity by widening or changing his economic activity, it also prevented people from performing certain services for themselves, e.g. shaving, hairdressing, sweeping the floor, or doing one's own laundry. By Western standards, job demarcations were not only too rigid and too fine, but some jobs were largely redundant. One might think that some of the lowest productivity occupations were invented simply to provide everyone with a job in a surplus labour situation, but there was no shortage of land and the productivity of the economy would have been higher if there had been greater job mobility. On economic criteria, the caste system must get very low marks. There was no allowance for aptitude, intelligence, or new ideas in allocating jobs; actual work performance had more ritual than functional significance, and it was impossible to fire anybody for inefficiency.

The caste system did not simply allocate jobs, it also defined the hierarchy of social precedence. In the middle ranges, the hierarchy was somewhat ambiguous, but the unequal status of untouchables was sharply demarcated by barriers of ritual impurity. Outcastes were not allowed in the same temples, nor could they use the same wells or burial grounds as caste Hindus. They lived in separate ghettos outside the main village, and in extreme cases could not approach within sixty-four feet of a caste Hindu. Any physical contact with them was regarded as polluting, and they were expected to adopt an attitude of cringing servility to their superiors. Outcastes in Southern India were not allowed to wear shoes, carry umbrellas, or to live in brick houses, and their women were not allowed to wear upper garments.[2] In pursuit of ritual purity, caste Hindus would not sweep floors, remove excrement or garbage. They left dirt till sweepers were available and the latter were invariably perfunctory in performing their pre-ordained tasks. Paradoxically, 'purity' became the enemy of hygiene, and Indian squalor was without parallel.

The caste system provided job security and allocated economic functions in a stable fashion in a society with no church hierarchy

[1] The changes which economic growth has brought to the traditional division of labour are described by O. Lewis, *Village Life in Northern India*, Random House, New York, 1958.

[2] See A. Beteille, *Castes Old and New*, Asia Publishing House, Bombay, 1969, p. 115.

and an unstable political system. It succeeded in imposing sanctions which held village society together for millennia, and it offered economic conditions and social status which were tolerable for the majority of inhabitants. The strength of village society was that it avoided extreme polarization of economic interests, and gave a portion of the community some stake in the economy, and an inferior group it could look down upon. Untouchables had a sub-human position, but the barrier of pollution prevented them making common cause with the lower grades of caste Hindus, and they were too debilitated and too small a minority to stage a successful rebellion. The disadvantages of this system were that it made for a low level of productivity, prevented innovation in production techniques and inhibited investment.

Another characteristic feature of Indian society was the joint family system. This system is common to many countries, and is useful in providing a considerable degree of social security. All generations of the family lived together and pooled their income with little distinction between brothers and cousins in terms of family obligations. However, the system inhibited individual incentives to work or save, and provided no motive for limiting family size. In the Indian joint family, women were completely subordinate to men, and adult men were expected to do what their fathers told them. Brides were not selected by husbands, but by the family. Husbands were normally considerably older than wives, but widows were not allowed to remarry and were expected to live in complete seclusion, even though their marriage might never have been consummated.

This kind of village society was the base of economic life for more than 2,000 years. Villages were defensive, self-contained units designed for survival in periods of war and alien domination. They paid taxes to whoever held state power, and were relatively indifferent to the passage of foreign invaders and rulers. Conquerors of India found a ready-made source of income, so they had no incentive to destroy the system. Instead they simply established themselves as a new and separate caste. The latter was the choice exercised by both the Muslims and the British. Newcomers to India did not merge into a homogeneous culture as they did in China, they simply became a new layer in the hierarchy of caste.

In addition to village society, India also had a large number of tribal communities. Aboriginal tribes led an independent pagan existence as hunters and forest dwellers, completely outside Hindu society and paying no taxes to the Moghuls. In present-day India, they are less than 7 per cent of the population. In the Moghul period their relative size was probably slightly larger.

Relations between Muslims and Hindus

At the height of its power under Akbar, the Moghul Empire[1] exercised religious toleration. This is one of the reasons why it was more successful in maintaining an extensive domain than the earlier Muslim sultanates of Delhi. There were some attempts to fuse Islamic doctrine with Hinduism, of which the main one was the Sikh religion, but this had a very limited success and Sikhs are still only 1 per cent of the population of the subcontinent. There was some interpenetration of religious practices, with the Muslims adopting saints and holy men, and the Hindus accepting purdah and the segregation of women. Indian Muslims also retained elements of caste which are inconsistent with a strict interpretation of Islamic principles. They had a system of endogamy within their own *biraderi* or tribal groups, and within their village communities some occupations tended to be hereditary. They also looked down upon sweepers, although their ideas about pollution were not as strong as those of Hindus. Finally, Muslims descended from immigrants looked down on Hindu converts.[2] In effect, the Muslim rulers did not succeed in creating an integrated society, but simply imposed themselves on top of the Hindus as a new caste segregated by different dietary and social habits, with a ban on marriage to infidels.

The Muslim population was always a minority but in the Moghul period it had probably become about a fifth or a quarter of the total. A minority of Indian Muslims (about 10 per cent) were descended from the Islamic conquerors (Turks, Afghans and Mongols) who had come to India via the Khyber Pass. The rest included some forcibly converted Hindus, and many more voluntary converts—low-caste Hindus attracted by the more egalitarian Muslim society. The Muslim ratio grew over time because polygamy and widow remarriage gave them greater fertility than Hindus. Muslims were highly concentrated in the North, in the Indo-Gangetic plain. In the South they were mainly in court towns and much more thinly spread. The first Muslim invaders carried out forcible conversions, but later rulers restrained their evangelizing activities partly because of Hindu resistance, partly because they realized that this would reduce their elite status. The only area where the indigenous population was converted to Islam *en masse* was East Bengal which had had a strong

[1] The Moghul emperors were Babur 1526–30, Humayun 1530–56 (whose reign was interrupted from 1540 to 1555 by the Afghans, Sher Shah and Islam Shah), Akbar 1556–1605, Jehangir 1605–27, Shah Jehan 1627–58, Aurangzeb 1658–1707. After Aurangzeb the Moghul Empire collapsed, though its nominal existence continued until 1857.

[2] See I. Ahmad, 'The Ashraf-Ajlaf Dichotomy in Muslim Social Structure in India', *The Indian Economic and Social History Review*, September 1966.

Buddhist tradition and looked on the Islamic invaders as liberators from Hindu rule.

Moghul control of India disintegrated after the death of Aurangzeb in 1707. Given the size of the country, which was as big as the whole of Europe, and its racial, linguistic and religious complexity, it is not surprising that it fell apart. Aurangzeb is often blamed for the collapse because he was too ambitious. He turned away from Akbar's policy of religious tolerance, destroyed Hindu temples, reimposed the *jizya* (a capitation tax on non-Muslims) and confiscated some non-Muslim princely states when titles lapsed. As a result Aurangzeb was engaged in a constant series of wars to hold his Empire together.[1] After his death, it split into several parts. In Western India, the Mahrattas established an independent Hindu state with their capital at Poona. The *Nizam-ul-Mulk*, a high Moghul official who foresaw the collapse of the Empire, installed himself as the autonomous ruler of Hyderabad in 1724. In 1739, the Persian emperor Nadir Shah invaded India, massacred the population of Delhi and took away so much booty (including Shah Jehan's peacock throne and the Kohinoor diamond) that he was able to remit Persian taxes for three years. He also annexed Punjab and set up an independent kingdom in Lahore. The Punjab was later captured by the Sikhs. In other areas which nominally remained in the Empire, e.g. Bengal, Mysore and Oudh, the power of the Moghul emperor declined, as did his revenue. Continuous internal warfare greatly weakened the economy and trade of the country.

It was because of these internal political and religious conflicts that the British were able to gain control of India. They exploited the differences skilfully by making temporary alliances and picking off local potentates one at a time. Many of their troops were local

---

[1] It has also been argued that the Moghul Empire declined because it had become too liberal under Akbar and that the Moghul collapse would have occurred earlier if it had not benefited from Aurangzeb's efforts to consolidate it religiously and to extend its area by military conquest. See I. H. Qureshi, *op. cit.*, p. 168: 'Akbar had strengthened his dynasty but made it subservient to interests other than those of Islam to a remarkable degree, so that it took three generations to restore the laws of Islam to their previous position. . . . Empires which are established by a numerically inferior community over a larger population always find themselves on the horns of a dilemma. They endure only so long as they can maintain the delicate balance between dominance and surrender. The difficulty with surrender is that it does not succeed unless it is complete. Akbar gave away so much, yet he was not able to reconcile the Hindu sentiment completely. . . . Conciliation, however deep, never takes the sting away from the sense of racial or national humiliation of the subject people. The best that such policies can achieve is the neutrality of large masses of people by looking after their interests.'

volunteers. They conquered the Moghul province of Bengal in 1757, took over the provinces of Madras and Bombay in 1803, and seized the Punjab from the Sikhs in 1848. The British government did not establish its own direct rule in India until 1857 when the East India Company was dissolved.

Conclusions

The Indian economy was the most complex and sophisticated to be colonized by Europeans, but its productivity level was significantly below that of Western Europe at the time of conquest in the mid-eighteenth century. Its relative backwardness was partly techno-logical but was mainly due to institutional characteristics which prevented it from making optimal use of its production possibilities.[1] The parasitic state apparatus had an adverse effect on production incentives in agriculture, which was reinforced by the effect of 'built-in depressants' within the village, where there was a further hierarchy of exploitation. Productive investment was negligible and the savings of the economy were invested in precious metals, palaces and tombs. The productivity of the urban economy was also adversely affected by the predatory character of the state. Urban industry and trade had less security against the arbitrary demands of the state than was the case in Western Europe. There were important Indian capitalists who operated as bankers and merchants, but international trade and part of the production of luxury handicrafts was in the hands of foreigners. The 'fiscal' levy supported a wealthy ruling class and a few specialized luxury goods industries. This economic surplus might later have been a source of rapid economic growth had it been mobilized by a modernizing elite, as happened in Meiji Japan, but in India (as we shall see in the next chapter) the fiscal surplus was whittled down, redistributed as rental income, and partially drained off in the colonial period.

Table II-1 gives a rough indication of the social structure of the Moghul Empire. It is based largely on the non-quantitative evidence

---

[1] I am not suggesting that the institutions of eighteenth-century Europe permitted optimal use of production possibilities. It is clear to any reader of Adam Smith that this was not the case. I am simply suggesting that the situation in India was worse than in Western Europe. In recent years, there has been a tendency to assume that all 'traditional societies' make optimal use of their production possibilities. T. W. Schultz is the main advocate of this viewpoint (see his *Transforming Traditional Agriculture*, Yale University Press, 1964) but his conclusions are too broad for the limited evidence he presents. He merely proves the more limited points that the marginal productivity of labour is not zero and that 'the economic acumen of people in poor agricultural communities is generally maligned'.

Table II-1

Social Structure of the Moghul Empire

Percentage of labour force		Percentage of national income after tax
18	NON-VILLAGE ECONOMY	52
1	Moghul Emperor and Court Mansabdars Jagirdars Native princes Appointed zamindars Hereditary zamindars	15
17	Merchants and bankers Traditional professions Petty traders and entrepreneurs Soldiers and petty bureaucracy Urban artisans and construction workers Servants Sweepers Scavengers	37
72	VILLAGE ECONOMY	45
	Dominant castes Cultivators and rural artisans Landless labourers Servants Sweepers Scavengers	
10	TRIBAL ECONOMY	3

cited in this chapter, and backward extrapolation from Table III-4 using the evidence cited in Chapter III. Although the basis for the estimates is shaky, there is some advantage in making explicit the orders of magnitude which are implicit in the argument of this chapter. If Tables II-1 and III-4 are compared it can be seen that the governmental oligarchy got a much larger share of national income in the Moghul period than under colonial rule, and village society got less, even though it probably contributed a little more to the total output of the economy in the earlier period. I have not felt able to allocate shares within the village economy, but they were probably less unequal than at the end of British rule. The heavier tax squeeze in the Moghul period almost certainly made its greatest impact on the upper income groups in the village. I have assumed that the tribal population was 10 per cent of the total as compared with 7 per cent at the end of British rule.

Chapter III

The Economic and Social Impact
of Colonial Rule

British imperialism was more pragmatic than that of other colonial powers. Its motivation was economic, not evangelical. There was none of the dedicated Christian fanaticism which the Portuguese and Spanish demonstrated in Latin America and less enthusiasm for cultural diffusion than the French (or the Americans) showed in their colonies. For this reason they Westernized India only to a limited degree.

British interests were of several kinds. At first the main purpose was to achieve a monopolistic trading position. Later it was felt that a regime of free trade would make India a major market for British goods and a source of raw materials, but British capitalists who invested in India, or who sold banking or shipping services there, continued effectively to enjoy monopolistic privileges. India also provided interesting and lucrative employment for a sizeable portion of the British upper middle class, and the remittances they sent home made an appreciable contribution to Britain's balance of payments and capacity to save. Finally, control of India was a key element in the world power structure, in terms of geography, logistics and military manpower. The British were not averse to Indian economic development if it increased their markets but refused to help in areas where they felt there was conflict with their own economic interests or political security. Hence, they refused to give protection to the Indian textile industry until its main competitor became Japan rather than Manchester, and they did almost nothing to further technical education. They introduced some British concepts of property, but did not push them too far when they met vested interests.

The main changes which the British made in Indian society were at the top. They replaced the wasteful warlord aristocracy by a bureaucratic-military establishment, carefully designed by utilitarian technocrats, which was very efficient in maintaining law and order. The greater efficiency of government permitted a substantial reduction in the fiscal burden, and a bigger share of the national product was available for landlords, capitalists and the new professional classes. Some of this upper class income was siphoned off to the

35

U.K., but the bulk was spent in India. However, the pattern of consumption changed as the new upper class no longer kept harems and palaces, nor did they wear fine muslins and damascened swords. This caused some painful readjustments in the traditional handicraft sector. It seems likely that there was some increase in productive investment which must have been near zero in Moghul India: government itself carried out productive investment in railways and irrigation and as a result there was a growth in both agricultural and industrial output. The new elite established a Western life-style using the English language and English schools. New towns and urban amenities were created with segregated suburbs and housing for them. Their habits were copied by the new professional elite of lawyers, doctors, teachers, journalists and businessmen. Within this group, old caste barriers were eased and social mobility increased.

As far as the mass of the population were concerned, colonial rule brought few significant changes. The British educational effort was very limited. There were no major changes in village society, in the caste system, the position of untouchables, the joint family system, or in production techniques in agriculture.

British impact on economic and social development was, therefore, limited. Total output and population increased substantially but the gain in *per capita* output was small or negligible.

It is interesting to speculate about India's potential economic fate if it had not had two centuries of British rule. There are three major alternatives which can be seriously considered. One would have been the maintenance of indigenous rule with a few foreign enclaves, as in China. Given the fissiparous forces in Indian society, it is likely that there would have been major civil wars as in China in the second half of the nineteenth century and the first half of the twentieth century and the country would probably have split up. Without direct foreign interference with its educational system, it is less likely that India would have developed a modernizing intelligentsia than China, because Indian society was less rational and more conservative, and the Chinese had a much more homogeneous civilization around which to build their reactive nationalism. If this situation had prevailed, population would certainly have grown less but the average standard of living might possibly have been a little higher because of the bigger upper class, and the smaller drain of resources abroad.[1]

[1] See A. Maddison, 'The Historical Origins of Indian Poverty', *Banca Nazionale del Lavoro Quarterly Review*, March 1970, which gives some comparative data on Indian and Chinese development in the colonial period. However, the comparison deserves much more detailed study. M. D. Morris has also speculated on the consequences of alternative paths of development, see his 'Trends and

Another alternative to British rule would have been conquest and maintenance of power by some other West European country such as France or Holland. This probably would not have produced results very different in economic terms from British rule. The third hypothesis is perhaps the most intriguing, i.e. conquest by a European power, with earlier accession to independence. If India had had self-government from the 1880s, after a century and a quarter of British rule, it is likely that both income and population growth would have been accelerated. There would have been a smaller drain of investible funds abroad, greater tariff protection, more state enterprise and favours to local industry, more technical training—the sort of things which happened after 1947. However, India would probably not have fared as well as Meiji Japan, because the fiscal leverage of government would have been smaller, zeal for mass education less, and religious and caste barriers would have remained as important constraints on productivity.

Establishment of a New Westernized Elite
The biggest change the British made in the social structure was to replace the warlord aristocracy by an efficient bureaucracy and army. The traditional system of the East India Company had been to pay its servants fairly modest salaries, and to let them augment their income from private transactions. This arrangement worked reasonably well before the conquest of Bengal, but was inefficient as a way of remunerating the officials of a substantial territorial Empire because (*a*) too much of the profit went into private hands rather than the Company's coffers, and (*b*) an over-rapacious short-term policy was damaging to the productive capacity of the economy and likely to drive the local population to revolt, both of which were against the Company's longer-term interests.

Clive had operated a 'dual' system, i.e. Company power and a

Tendencies in Indian Economic History', *The Indian Economic and Social History Review*, December 1968. Morris is the most outspoken critic of the 'canonical tradition' of Indian nationalist historians who have put great emphasis on colonialism as a cause of Indian poverty. His original article on this theme was 'Towards a Reinterpretation of Nineteenth Century Indian Economic History', *Journal of Economic History*, December 1963, was reprinted in the March 1968 issue of *The Indian Economic and Social History Review*, together with a reply by three critics, of which the most outstanding is Professor T. Raychaudhuri. My own feeling is that Morris does not emphasize sufficiently the retarding effect of 'the drain', understates the adverse impact of British conquest on luxury handicrafts, understates the role of caste as a hindrance to economic growth, and exaggerates the improvement in *per capita* income under British rule.

puppet Nawab. Warren Hastings displaced the Nawab and took over direct administration, but retained Indian officials. Finally, in 1785, Cornwallis created a professional cadre of Company servants who had generous salaries, had no private trading or production interests in India, enjoyed the prospect of regular promotion and were entitled to pensions.[1] All high-level posts were reserved for the British, and Indians were excluded. Cornwallis appointed British judges, and established British officials as revenue collectors and magistrates in each district of Bengal.

From 1806 the Company trained its young recruits in Haileybury College near London. Appointments were still organized on a system of patronage, but after 1833 the Company selected amongst its nominated candidates by competitive examination. After 1853, selection was entirely on merit and the examination was thrown open to any British candidate. The examination system was influenced by the Chinese model, which had worked well for 2,000 years and had a similar emphasis on classical learning and literary competence. The Indian civil service was therefore able to secure high quality people because (a) it was very highly paid; (b) it enjoyed political power which no bureaucrat could have had in England.

In 1829 the system was strengthened by establishing districts throughout British India small enough to be effectively controlled by an individual British official who henceforth exercised a completely autocratic power, acting as revenue collector, judge and chief of police (functions which had been separate under the Moghul administration). This arrangement later became the cornerstone of Imperial administration throughout the British Empire. As the civil service was ultimately subject to the control of the British parliament, and the British community in India was subject to close mutual surveillance, the administration was virtually incorruptible.

The army of the Company was a local mercenary force with 20,000–30,000 British officers and troops. It was by far the most modern and efficient army in Asia. After the Mutiny in 1857, the

---

[1] See *Report of the Pay and Services Commission*, 1959–62, Government of Pakistan, 1969, p. 23: 'The term "Civil Service" was used for the first time by the East India Company which maintained military forces side by side with a body of "merchants, factors and writers" exclusively recruited in England whose functions, with the onward march of the Company's administrative responsibilities, underwent a process of transformation into those of local administrators while the Company's trading activities gradually declined. Thus the civil administration of the country passed by degrees into the hands of those employees of the Company, whose careers were secured by the terms of covenants executed in England, before they left for India, and who were therefore known as Covenanted Servants of the Company.'

size of the British contingent was raised to a third of the total strength and all officers were British until the 1920s when a very small number of Indians was recruited. Normally, the total strength of the army was about 200,000. This army was very much smaller than those of Moghul India,[1] but had better training and equipment, and the railway network (which was constructed partly for military reasons) gave it greater mobility, better logistics and intelligence.

The higher ranks of the administration remained almost entirely British until the 1920s when the Indian civil service examinations began to be held in India as well as the U.K.[2] In addition, there was a whole hierarchy of separate bureaucracies in which the higher ranks were British, i.e. the revenue, justice, police, education, medical, public works, engineering, postal and railway services as well as the provincial civil services. India thus offered highly-paid careers to an appreciable portion of the British middle and upper classes (particularly for its peripheral members from Scotland and Ireland).

From the 1820s to the 1850s the British demonstrated a strong urge to change Indian social institutions, and to Westernize India.[3] They stamped out infanticide and ritual burning of widows (*sati*). They abolished slavery and eliminated *dacoits* (religious thugs) from the highways. They legalized the remarriage of widows and allowed Hindu converts to Christianity to lay claim to their share of joint family property. They took steps to introduce a penal code (the code was actually introduced in 1861) based on British law, which helped inculcate some ideas of equality. 'Under his old Hindu law, a Brahmin murderer might not be put to death, while a Sudra who cohabited with a high-caste woman would automatically suffer execution. Under the new law, Brahmin and Sudra were liable to the same punishment for the same offence.'[4]

There was a strong streak of Benthamite radicalism in the East

[1] Moreland suggests that in the time of Akbar the military strength of India was well over a million men, i.e. about four times the size of the armies maintained in British India and the princely states, and much bigger in relation to population. See W. H. Moreland, *India at the Death of Akbar*, A. Ram, Delhi, 1962, p. 72.

[2] The army officer class was more exclusive than the civil service and in 1911 had practically no Indians and only 135 Anglo-Indians as compared with 4,378 British officers, see *Census of India*, 1911. P. Woodruff, *The Men who Ruled India, The Guardians*, Cape, London, 1963, p. 363, shows the composition of the I.C.S. (the top rank of the civil service) from 1859 to 1939. In 1869 there were 882 Europeans and 1 Indian; in 1909, 1,082 Europeans and 60 Indians; in 1939, 759 Europeans and 540 Indians.

[3] See S. Sivasubramonian, *National Income of India 1900–1 to 1946–7*, Delhi School of Economics, 1965 (mimeographed).

[4] See H. Tinker, *India and Pakistan*, Pall Mall, London, 1967, p. 172.

India Company administration.[1] James Mill became a senior company official in 1819 after writing a monumental history of India which showed a strong contempt for Indian institutions.[2] From 1831 to 1836 he was the chief executive officer of the E.I.C. and his son John Stuart Mill worked for the Company from 1823 to 1858. Malthus was professor of economics at Haileybury, and the teaching there for future company officials was strongly influenced by Utilitarianism. Bentham himself was also consulted on the reform of Indian institutions. The Utilitarians deliberately used India to try out experiments and ideas (e.g. competitive entry for the civil service) which they would have liked to apply in England. The Utilitarians were strong supporters of *laissez-faire* and abhorred any kind of state interference to promote economic development. Thus they tended to rely on market forces to deal with famine problems, they did nothing to stimulate agriculture or protect industry. This *laissez-faire* tradition was more deeply embedded in the Indian civil service than in the U.K. itself, and persisted very strongly until the late 1920s. The administration was efficient and incorruptible, but the state apparatus was of a watchdog character with few development ambitions. Even in 1936, more than half of government spending was for the military, justice, police and jails, and less than 3 per cent for agriculture.[3]

One of the most significant things the British did to Westernize India was to introduce a modified version of English education. Macaulay's 1835 Minute on Education had a decisive impact on British educational policy and is a classic example of a Western rationalist approach to Indian civilization. Before the British took over, the Court language of the Moghuls was Persian and the Muslim population used Urdu, a mixture of Persian, Arabic and

[1] See E. Stokes, *The English Utilitarians and India*, Oxford, 1959, for an analysis of their influence.

[2] *Ibid.*, p. 53: 'James Mill's *History of British India* was principally an attempt to make a philosophic analysis of Indian society and assess its place in the "scale of civilization". Undoubtedly one of his main aims was to dispel what he considered the silly sentimental admiration of oriental despotism which had marked the earlier thinkers of the Enlightenment. Even such a "keen-eyed and skeptical judge" as Voltaire had succumbed, and the conservative tendencies of the Enlightenment had been mischievously strengthened. Mill's indictment of so-called Hindu and Muslim civilization is a *tour de force*. . . . In India there was a "hideous state of society", much inferior in acquirements to Europe even in its darkest feudal age. So far from any diffidence on account of his entire lack of personal experience of India, Mill prided himself that the severity of his judgement was all the more justified by its very disinterestedness.'

[3] See V. Anstey, *The Economic Development of India*, Longmans Green, London, 1952, p. 540.

Sanskrit. Higher education was largely religious and stressed know-ledge of Arabic and Sanskrit. The Company had given some financial support to a Calcutta Madrassa (1781), and a Sanskrit college at Benares (1792). Warren Hastings, as governor general from 1782 to 1795 had himself learned Sanskrit and Persian, and several other Company officials were oriental scholars. One of them, Sir William Jones, had translated a great mass of Sanskrit literature and had founded the Asiatic Society of Bengal in 1785. But Macaulay was strongly opposed to this orientalism:

'I believe that the present system tends, not to accelerate the progress of truth, but to delay the natural death of expiring errors. We are a Board for wasting public money, for printing books which are less value than the paper on which they are printed was while it was blank; for giving artificial encouragement to absurd history, absurd metaphysics, absurd physics, absurd theology. . . . I have no knowledge of either Sanskrit or Arabic. . . . But I have done what I could to form a correct estimate of their value. . . . Who could deny that a single shelf of a good European library was worth the whole native literature of India and Arabia . . . all the historical information which has been collected from all the books written in the Sanskrit language is less valuable than what may be found in the most paltry abridgements used at preparatory schools in England.'

For these reasons Macaulay had no hesitation in deciding in favour of English education, but it was not to be for the masses:

'It is impossible for us, with our limited means to attempt to educate the body of the people. We must at present do our best to form a class who may be interpreters between us and the millions whom we govern; a class of persons, Indian in blood and colour, but English in taste, in opinions, in morals, and in intellect. To that class we may leave it to refine the vernacular dialects of the country, to enrich those dialects with terms of science borrowed from the Western nomenclature, and to render them by degrees fit vehicles for conveying knowledge to the great mass of the population.'[1]

Until 1857 it was possible to entertain the view (as Marx did)[2]

[1] Quoted from the text as given in M. Edwardes, *British India 1772–1947*, Sidgwick and Jackson, London, 1967.
[2] See K. Marx, article in the *New York Daily Tribune*, August 8, 1853: 'England has to fulfil a double mission in India: one destructive, the other regenerating— the annihilation of old Asiatic society, and the laying of the material foundations

that the British might eventually destroy traditional Indian society and Westernize the country. But activist Westernizing policies and the attempt to extend British rule by taking over native states whose rulers had left no heirs provoked sections of both the Hindu and Muslim communities into rebellion in the Mutiny of 1857. Although the Mutiny was successfully put down with substantial help from loyal Indian troops including the recently conquered Sikhs, British policy towards Indian institutions and society became much more conservative. The Crown took over direct responsibility and the East India Company was disbanded. The Indian civil service attracted fewer people with innovating ideas than had the East India Company and was more closely controlled from London. The British forged an alliance with the remaining native princes and stopped taking over new territory. Until the end of their rule about a quarter of the Indian population remained in quasi-autonomous native states. These had official British residents but were fairly free in internal policy, and the effort of Westernization came to a standstill.

The education system which developed was a very pale reflection of that in the U.K. Three universities were set up in 1857 in Calcutta, Madras and Bombay, but they were merely examining bodies and did no teaching. Higher education was carried out in affiliated colleges which gave a two-year B.A. course with heavy emphasis on rote learning and examinations. Drop-out ratios were always very high. They did little to promote analytic capacity or independent thinking and produced a group of graduates with a half-baked knowledge of English, but sufficiently Westernized to be alienated from their own culture.[1] It was not until the 1920s that Indian universities provided teaching facilities and then only for M.A. students. Furthermore, Indian education was of a predominantly literary character and the provision for technical training was much

---

of Western society in Asia.' In his articles on India, Marx stressed the fact that the British were breaking up the village community, uprooting handicraft industry, and establishing private property in land—'the great desideratum of Indian society'. He also expected irrigation and railways to have a significant effect on economic growth, and that industrialization would destroy the caste system: 'Modern industry, resulting from the railway system, will dissolve the hereditary divisions of labour, upon which rest the Indian castes, those decisive impediments to Indian progress and Indian power.' Marx's assessment of the likely impact of British rule was reasonable enough in 1853 when it was written, but unfortunately these brief newspaper articles (which Marx based largely on information provided by Engels) have been resuscitated by vulgar Marxists as if they were holy writ, particularly by Palme Dutt. Thus they have contributed to the general exaggeration of the impact of British rule in India.

[1] See Government of India, *Report of the Education Commission 1964–66*, Delhi, 1966.

less than in any European country. Education for girls was almost totally ignored throughout the nineteenth century. Because higher education was in English, there was no official effort to translate Western literature into the vernacular, nor was there any standardization of Indian scripts whose variety is a major barrier to multilingualism amongst educated Indians.

Primary education was not taken very seriously as a government obligation and was financed largely by the weak local authorities. As a result, the great mass of the population had no access to education and, at independence in 1947, 88 per cent were illiterate. Progress was accelerated from the 1930s onwards, but at independence only a fifth of children were receiving any primary schooling.

Education could have played a major role in encouraging social mobility, eliminating religious superstition, increasing productivity, and uplifting the status of women. Instead it was used to turn a tiny elite into imitation Englishmen and a somewhat bigger group into government clerks.

Having failed to Westernize India, the British established themselves as a separate ruling caste. Like other Indian castes, they did not intermarry or eat with the lower (native) castes. Thanks to the British public-school system, their children were shipped off and did not mingle with the natives. At the end of their professional careers they returned home. The small creole class of Anglo-Indians were outcastes unable to integrate into Indian or local British society.[1] The British kept to their clubs and bungalows in special suburbs known as cantonments and civil lines. They maintained the Moghul tradition of official pomp, sumptuary residences, and retinues of servants.[2] They did not adopt the Moghul custom of polygamy, but remained monogamous and brought in their own women. Society became prim and priggish.[3] The British ruled India in much the same

[1] The situation was totally different in the Portuguese colony of Goa. The Portuguese intermarried with the natives, broke down caste barriers, brought in Jesuit priests, imposed Catholicism, imported a saint, buried him locally and thus established a centre for pilgrimage. Spanish practice in the Philippines was similar. The British deliberately kept out missionaries until 1813, which is when they brought in their first bishop.

[2] See Lord Beveridge's life of his parents, *India Called Them*, Allen and Unwin, London, 1957. Beveridge's father did not have a very successful career, but had 21 servants to start married life, 39 when he had three children, and 18 when living on his own. The 18 servants cost him less than 6 per cent of his salary.

[3] The change in British attitudes in the early nineteenth century is noted in M. Edwardes, *op. cit.*, p. 33. 'There were other factors which contributed to the growing estrangement between Indians and the British. One of these was the growing number of women in the British settlements. They tended to bring with

way as the Roman consuls had ruled in Africa 2,000 years earlier, and were very conscious of the Roman paradigm. The elite with its classical education and contempt for business were quite happy establishing law and order, and keeping 'barbarians' at bay on the frontier of the raj.[1] They developed their own brand of self-righteous arrogance, considering themselves purveyors not of popular but of good government. For them. the word 'British' lost its geographic connotation and became an epithet signifying moral rectitude.

The striking thing about the British raj is that it was operated by so few people. There were only 31,000 British in India in 1805 (of which 22,000 were in the army and 2,000 in civil government).[2] The number increased substantially after the Mutiny, but thereafter remained steady. In 1911, there were 164,000 British (106,000 employed, of which 66,000 were in the army and police and 4,000 in civil government).[3] In 1931, there were 168,000 (90,000 employed, 60,000 in the army and police and 4,000 in civil government). They were a thinner layer than the Muslim rulers had been (never more than 0·05 per cent of the population).

Because of the small size of the administration and its philosophy of minimal government responsibility outside the field of law and order, India ended the colonial period with a very low level of

---

them the prejudices of their time. Their attitude, generally speaking, was Christian, and narrowly so. They brought, too, a new sense of family life, and their arrival resulted in the expulsion of native mistresses who had at least injected something of India into the world of the British. The women had little to occupy their minds. Their life was a tedious social round. But they did have gossip.'

[1] The connections with India had a substantial impact on British domestic institutions and attitudes. The British civil service, with its tradition of generalists and brahminical status of the administrative class, is derived from the Indian model. The British 'public' school system was greatly strengthened by the needs of expatriate families. The domestic status of royalty was enhanced by the Imperial connection. The close contact with Hindu casteism strengthened British snobbery and helped to make the British somewhat more racist towards subject peoples than the French and Dutch who intermarried with colonials much more.

[2] See D. A. B. Bhattacharya (ed.), *Report on the Population Estimates of Inda*, *(1820–30)*, *Census of India 1961*, Government of India, Registrar General, Delhi, 1963, pp. 4–5.

[3] See *Census of India 1911*, Vol. I, *India*, Part II, *Tables*, Calcutta, 1913, pp. 374–6. The total population of all India (including native states) was 313 million and the total labour force 149 million. It is interesting to note that the European population of India was of relatively much lower importance than in Indonesia, where there were 81,000 Europeans in a population of 38 million in 1905: see J. S. Furnivall, *Colonial Policy and Practice*, Cambridge, 1948, p. 255; or in French Indo-China with 42,000 Europeans and a total population of 23 million in 1937: see C. Robequain, *The Economic Development of French Indo-China*, Oxford University Press, London, 1944.

taxation. The British had inherited the Moghul tax system which provided a land revenue equal to 15 per cent of national income, but by the end of the colonial period land tax was only 1 per cent of national income and the total tax burden was only 6 per cent. It is curious that this large reduction in the fiscal burden has passed almost without comment in the literature on Indian economic history.[1] On the contrary, emphasis is usually placed on the heaviness of the tax burden, e.g. by D. Naoroji and R. C. Dutt.

Most of the benefits of the lower fiscal burden were felt by landlords, and were not passed on to the mass of the population. In urban areas new classes emerged under British rule, i.e. industrial capitalists and a new bourgeoisie of bureaucrats, lawyers, doctors, teachers and journalists whose social position was due to education and training rather than heredity. In the princely states, the remnants of the Moghul aristocracy continued their extravagances—large palaces, harems, hordes of retainers, miniature armies, ceremonial elephants, tiger hunts, and stables full of Rolls Royces.

Agriculture

The colonial government made institutional changes in agriculture by transforming traditionally circumscribed property rights into something more closely resembling the unencumbered private property characteristic of Western capitalism. The beneficiaries of these new rights varied in different parts of India. The top layer of Moghul property, the jagir, was abolished (except in the autonomous princely states), and the bulk of the old warlord aristocracy was dispossessed. Their previous income from land revenue, and that of the Moghul state, was now appropriated by the British as land tax. However, in the Bengal Presidency (i.e. modern Bengal, Bihar, Orissa and part of Madras) the second layer of Moghul property rights belonging to Moghul tax collectors (zamindars) was reinforced.[2] All zamindars in these areas now had hereditary status,[3] so long as they paid their land taxes, and their judicial and administrative functions disappeared. In the Moghul period the zamindars had

[1] Tapan Raychaudhuri is the only Indian historian to have stressed this point. See his essay in R. E. Frykenberg (ed.), *Land Control and Social Structure in Indian History*, Madison, 1969, p. 168: 'the relatively low and unchanging rate of revenue demand which left a large surplus to be distributed among a numerous and parasitical class of rather poor intermediaries'.

[2] Big Moghul landlords (taluqdars) were also confirmed in their position in Oudh (U.P.) after the Mutiny of 1857.

[3] Even in the Moghul period many zamindars had held hereditary status because they were from Hindu families which had been local chieftains in pre-Moghul times. Other zamindars had lifetime status.

usually kept a tenth of the land revenue to themselves, but by the end of British rule their income from rents was a multiple of the tax they paid to the state. In Bihar, for instance, five-sixths of the total sum levied by 1950 was rent and only one-sixth revenue.[1] However, zamindars were not really the equivalent of Western landowners. Dominant families in each village remained as their 'tenants-in-chief' and continued to enjoy many of the old customary rights, i.e. they could not be evicted, their rights were heritable and their rental payments could not be raised easily. Lower-caste families were usually sub-tenants of the tenants-in-chief, rather than direct tenants of the zamindars. Often there were several layers of tenancy between the actual cultivator and the zamindar. Sub-tenants had less security and less defence against rack-renting than tenants-in-chief. It is worth noting that when zamindari rights were abolished around 1952 and the old zamindar rental income was converted into state revenue, the amount involved was only about 2 per cent of farm income in the relevant areas of India. This suggests that by the end of the colonial period, the zamindars were not able to squeeze as much surplus out of their chief tenants as is sometimes suggested.

The typical zamindari estate at the end of British rule seems to have been very different from that at the end of the eighteenth century. In Bengal the total 'number of landowners which did not exceed 100 in the beginning of Hasting's administration in 1772, rose in the course of a century to 154,200'. In 1872 there were 154,200 estates of which '533, or 0·34 per cent, only are great properties with an area of 20,000 acres and upwards; 15,747, or 10·21 per cent, range from 500 to 20,000 acres in area; while the number of estates which fell short of 500 acres is no less than 137,920, or 89·44 per cent, of the whole'.[2]

Misra attributes this fall in the average size of zamindari properties to the fact that they could be inherited or sold freely, whereas the Moghul state wanted to keep the number small because zamindars had administrative functions under the Moghul Empire. Under the British, transfers became much more frequent, particularly into the

---

[1] See D. Warriner, *Land Reform in Principle and Practice*, Oxford University Press, 1969, p. 158.

[2] See B. B. Misra, *op. cit.*, p. 131. Nehru made the same point about zamindars in the United Provinces. See J. Nehru, *An Autobiography*, Allied Publishers, Bombay, 1962, p. 58: 'In the United Provinces, so far as I can remember, there are a million-and-a-half persons classed as zamindars. Probably over ninety per cent of these are almost on the same level as the poorest tenants, and another nine per cent are only moderately well off. The biggish landowners are not more than five thousand in the whole province, and of this number, about one-tenth might be considered the really big zamindars and taluqadars.'

hands of moneylenders. The moneylenders are frequently presented as squeezing out poor peasants and tenantry and thus promoting the concentration of wealth, but the evidence of what happened to zamindar estates suggests that village moneylenders may also have helped to break up concentrations of wealth.[1]

In the Madras and Bombay Presidencies, which covered most of Southern India, the British dispossessed many of the old Moghul and Mahratta nobility and big zamindars, and vested property rights and tax obligations in individual 'peasants'. This settlement was known as the *ryotwari* (peasant tenure) system. However, the term peasant is misleading, because most of those who acquired land titles belonged to the traditionally dominant castes in villages. Lower-caste cultivators became their tenants. Thus there was no change in social structure at the village level, except that the new ownership rights gave greater opportunities for sale and mortgage, and the security of the tenant was less than it had been under the previous system. The change in legal status was limited by several factors. First of all, illiterate peasants did not always understand the new situation, and there were strong social ties in the joint family and the caste panchayats to prevent major deviations from old habits. Secondly, the new administration was rather remote from individual villages (with a district officer responsible for over a thousand villages), and many British administrators had a personal bias in favour of customary tenant rights because by maintaining them they could avoid political trouble. At a later stage, the government itself introduced a good deal of legislation to protect customary rights in response to peasant disturbances.[2] Land policy was, therefore, another instance of British policy of half-Westernization. The change from custom to contract was not nearly as sharp as that brought about in Japan by the Meiji land reforms. The British were more concerned with arrangements which would guarantee their revenue and not provoke too much political disturbance rather than in increasing productivity or introducing capitalist institutions. The Utilitarians who dominated the Company from 1820 to 1850 would have liked to push in this direction, but they were displaced at mid-century by the paternalist conservatives of the Imperial raj.

Nevertheless, there were some economic consequences of the new legal situation. Because of the emergence of clear titles, it was now

[1] See W. C. Neale, *Economic Change in Rural India*, Yale University Press, 1962, p. 63.
[2] e.g. the Bengal Act X of 1859, the Bengal Tenancy Act of 1885, the Oudh Sub-Settlement Act of 1866, the Deccan Agriculturalists Relief Act of 1879 and the Punjab Alienation of Land Act of 1900.

possible to mortgage land. The status of moneylenders was also improved by the change from Muslim to British law. There had been moneylenders in the Moghul period, but their importance grew substantially under British rule, and over time a considerable amount of land changed hands through foreclosures[1].

Over time, two forces raised the income of landowners. One of these was the increasing scarcity of land as population expanded. This raised land values and rents. The second was the decline in the incidence of land tax. Indian literature usually stresses the heavy burden of land tax in the early days of British rule,[2] but the fact that it fell substantially over time is seldom noted. The Moghul land tax was about 30 per cent of the crop, but by 1947 land tax was only 2 per cent of agricultural income. The fall was most marked in Bengal where the tax was fixed in perpetuity in 1793, but it was also true in other areas.

As a result of these changes, there was not only an increase in village income but a widening of income inequality within villages. The village squirearchy received relatively higher incomes because of the reduced burden of land tax and the increase in rents; tenants and agricultural labourers may well have experienced a decline in income because their traditional rights were curtailed and their bargaining power was reduced by land scarcity. The class of landless agricultural labourers grew in size under British rule, but modern scholarship[3] has shown that they were not a 'creation' of the British.

[1] For a description of the changed status of the moneylender under British rule, see M. L. Darling, *The Punjab Peasant in Prosperity and Debt*, Oxford University Press, London, 1947, p. 178: 'For centuries he was nothing but a servile adjunct to the Mohammadan cultivator, who despised him as much for his trade as for his religion. Forbidden to wear a turban and allowed to ride only on a donkey, and often the object of "unmentionable indignities", sufferance was the badge of all his tribe; but when British rule freed him from restraint and armed him with the power of the law, he became as oppressive as he had hitherto been submissive.'

[2] See particularly R. C. Dutt, *op. cit.* Dutt was a spokesman of landlord interests who argued strongly against 'excessive' land taxation. He was one of the early leaders of the nationalist movement whose spurious arguments still unfortunately carry some weight.

[3] See D. Kumar, *Land and Caste in South India*, Cambridge, 1965, who estimates that landless labourers were 15 per cent of the rural population of South India in 1800. Mrs Kumar's book reviews the extensive literature which attempts to show that the British created the class of landless labourers. Her critique of R. P. Dutt, *India Today*, is particularly devastating. Dutt asserts that: 'In 1842 Sir Thomas Munro, as Census Commissioner, reported that there were no landless peasants in India.' Mrs Kumar retorts: 'It does not strengthen one's confidence in this view to recall that there was no all-India census until 1871, that there was no Madras census in 1842, that Sir Thomas Munro was never Census Commissioner, and that in 1842 he was dead.'

They were about 15 per cent of the rural population at the end of the eighteenth century, and about a quarter of the labour force now.

Although these were important modifications in the village structure, the traditional hierarchy of caste was not destroyed. Income differentials widened, but the social and ritual hierarchy in villages did not change its character. Village society was not egalitarian in Moghul times, and in most cases those whose income rose in the British period were already socially dominant, although there were exceptions.[1] Recent sociological studies, although they indicate changes in the British period, also portray a village hierarchy in the 1940s and 1950s which cannot be very different from that in the Moghul period.[2] We still find a dominant caste of petty landlords, an intermediate group of tenants, village artisans tied by jajmani relationships, a group of low-status labourers, untouchable menials with the whole held together by the same elaborate system of caste.

One might have expected the legal changes introduced by the British to have had a positive effect on efficiency. They removed the class of jagirdars who had no incentive to invest in agriculture, and gave land rights to rural capitalists who could buy and sell land fairly freely and enjoy an increasing portion of the product. Moneylenders helped to root out improvident or inefficient landowners. However, most farmers were illiterate and the government did not provide research or extension services, or encourage the use of fertilizers. Until recently, with the arrival of the tubewell, there were technical limits to the possibility of small-scale irrigation. There were also organizational difficulties in changing technique to improve productivity. The division of labour in the village and hereditary attitudes to work as a semi-religious ritual rather than a means to improve income were obstacles to change. Furthermore, a good many of the cultivating landowners whose income was increased were relatively poor and used their increased income for consumption rather than investment. Some of those who were better off probably improved their land or took over waste land, but as religion inculcated the idea that manual labour was polluting, some of them probably worked less.[3] The big zamindars used some of their extra income to develop waste land, but many cultivated a life style rather like the old Moghul aristocracy and had a high propensity to consume.

[1] See F. G. Bailey, op. cit.

[2] See M. Marriott (ed.), Village India, Chicago, 1955; O. Lewis, op. cit.; M. N. Srinivas (ed.), India's Villages, Asia Publishing House, Bombay, 1969.

[3] See D. Thorner, The Agrarian Prospect in India, Delhi School of Economics, 1956, p. 12: 'The primary aim of all classes in the agrarian structure has been not to increase their income by adopting more efficient methods, but to rise in social prestige by abstaining insofar as possible from physical labour.'

According to Raychaudhuri, 'a zamindar's house with a hundred rooms was not exceptional'.[1] Some of the enterprising ones probably transferred their savings out of agriculture into trade and industry or bought their children a Western-type education. Thus the effect of the change was to increase productivity and savings, but not much.

During the period of British rule, agricultural production grew substantially in order to feed a population which grew from 165 million in 1757 to 420 million in 1947. The new system of land ownership offered some stimulus to increase output, and there was substantial waste land available for development.

The colonial government made some contribution towards increased output through irrigation. The irrigated area was increased about eightfold, and eventually more than a quarter of the land of British India was irrigated.[2] Irrigation was extended both as a source of revenue and as a measure against famine. A good deal of the irrigation work was in the Punjab and Sind. The motive here was to provide land for retired Indian army personnel, many of whom came from the Punjab, and to build up population in an area which bordered on the disputed frontier with Afghanistan. These areas, which had formerly been desert, became the biggest irrigated area in the world and a major producer of wheat and cotton, both for export and for sale in other parts of India. Apart from government investment in irrigation, there was substantial private investment, and by the end of British rule private irrigation investment covered nearly 25 million acres of British India.

Improvements in transport facilities (particularly railways, but also steamships and the Suez canal) helped agriculture by permitting some degree of specialization on cash crops. This increased yields somewhat, but the bulk of the country stuck to subsistence farming. Plantations were developed for indigo, sugar, jute and tea. These items made a significant contribution to exports, but in the context of Indian agriculture as a whole, they were not very important. In 1946, the two primary staples, tea and jute, were less than 3·5 per cent of the gross value of crop output.[3] Thus the enlargement of

[1] See T. Raychaudhuri, 'Permanent Settlement in Operation: Bakarganj District, East Bengal' in R. E. Frykenberg (ed.), *Land Control and Social Structure in Indian History*, Madison, 1969.

[2] See *The First Five Year Plan*, Planning Commission, Delhi, December, 1952, pp. 338 and 344. In 1850, 2 to 3 million acres were irrigated by tank or canal and 5 million acres by wells. In 1941–5, 58·1 million out of 216·6 million acres of cultivated land in British India were irrigated of which 33·6 million acres by government works.

[3] See G. Blyn, *Agricultural Trends in India, 1891–1947*, University of

markets through international trade was less of a stimulus in India than in other Asian countries such as Ceylon, Burma or Thailand.[1]

Little was done to promote agricultural technology. There was some improvement in seeds, but no extension service, no improvement in livestock and no official encouragement to use fertilizer. Lord Mayo, the Governor General, said in 1870, 'I do not know what is precisely meant by ammoniac manure. If it means guano, superphosphate or any other artificial product of that kind, we might as well ask the people of India to manure their ground with champagne.'[2]

Statistics are not available on agricultural output for the first century and a half of British rule, but all the indications suggest that there was substantial growth. We do not know whether output rose faster or more slowly than population, but it seems likely that the movements were roughly parallel.

For the last half century of British rule, the main calculations of output are those by George Blyn. His first study, which has been widely quoted, was published in 1954 by the National Income Unit of the Indian government, and showed only a 3 per cent increase in crop output in British India from 1893 to 1946, i.e. a period in which population increased 46 per cent! His second study, published in 1966 showed a 16·6 per cent increase, and this, too, has been widely quoted, but he also gives a 'modified' series which shows a 28·9 per cent increase. This seems preferable, as the official figures on rice yields in Orissa, which are corrected in his 'modified' estimate, seem obviously in error. However, even Blyn's upper estimate is probably an understatement because he shows a very small increase in acreage. It is difficult to believe that *per capita* food output could have gone down as much as he suggests, whilst waste land remained unused. There has been a very big increase in the cultivated area since independence and it seems likely that the increase in the preceding

---

Pennsylvania, 1966. These two items were about 5·2 per cent of the eighteen crops he lists, but he covers only about 62 per cent of total crops.

[1] In Ceylon tea, rubber, coconuts and other estate crops were three-quarters of agricultural output in 1950, see D. R. Snodgrass, *Ceylon: An Export Economy in Transition*, Irwin, Illinois, 1966, p. 128. In Thailand rice exports rose from 5 per cent of output in 1905 to 50 per cent in 1907, see J. C. Ingram, *Economic Change in Thailand since 1850*, Stanford, 1955. For theoretical analysis of the impact of trade and colonization on South-East Asia, see H. Myint, 'The Classical Theory of International Trade and the Underdeveloped Countries', *Economic Journal*, June 1958, and R. E. Caves ' "Vent for Surplus" Models of Trade and Growth', in R. E. Caves, H. G. Johnson, and P. B. Kenen, *Trade Growth and Balance of Payments*, North Holland, Amsterdam, 1965.

[2] See M. Edwardes, *op. cit.*, p. 219.

half century was bigger than Blyn suggests. Therefore, my own estimate of crop output (Appendix B) for 1900–46, uses Blyn's figures on yields but assumes that the cultivated area rose by 23 per cent (Sivasubramonian's figure) rather than by 12·2 per cent (Blyn's figure).[1] My estimate shows agricultural output rising about the same amount as population from 1900 to 1946. However, even this may be too low.

The basic reports on areas under cultivation are those provided by village accountants (*patwaris*) in areas where land revenue was periodically changed, and by village watchmen (*chowkidars*) in areas where the land revenue was permanently settled. There was some incentive for farmers to bribe patwaris to under-report land for tax purposes, and chowkidars are all too often illiterate and drowsy people, who would usually report that things were normal, i.e. the same as the year before. There is, therefore, a tendency for under-reporting of both levels and rates of growth in areas covered by statistics, and the areas not covered by statistics were generally on the margin of cultivation and may have had a more steeply rising trend than the average area covered. Thus Blyn shows no growth in output in Bengal where the chowkidars did the basic reporting. He did not cover the Sind desert area in which the British built the huge Sukkur barrage in 1932. Blyn was, of course, aware of these difficulties and tried to correct for them as far as possible, but the fundamental problems are not amenable to 'statistical' manipulation but require 'hunch' adjustment.

My own conclusion from the evidence available is that agricultural output per head was at least as high at the end of British rule as it was in the Moghul period, and that rural consumption levels were somewhat higher because of the lower tax burden on agriculture, and the smaller degree of wastage which allowed surplus areas to sell their grains. This slight improvement in standards may have contributed to the expansion in population. However, agricultural yields and nutritional levels at independence were amongst the lowest in the world.

Under British rule, the Indian population remained subject to recurrent famines and epidemic diseases. In 1876–8 and 1899–1900 famine killed millions of people. In the 1890s there was a widespread outbreak of bubonic plague and in 1919 a great influenza epidemic. It is sometimes asserted by Indian nationalist historians that British policy increased the incidence of famine in India,[2] particularly in the

---

[1] See G. Blyn, *op. cit.*, pp. 251, 316–17 and 349–50, which gives his first, second and modified estimates. For my estimates, see Appendix B.

[2] This is the argument of Romesh Dutt and also of the British author William

nineteenth century. Unfortunately we do not have any figures on agricultural production for this period, and it is difficult to base a judgement merely on catalogues of famine years whose intensity we cannot measure. As agriculture was extended to more marginal land one would have expected output to become more volatile. But this was offset to a considerable extent by the major improvement in transport brought by railways, and the greater security of water supply brought by irrigation. It is noteworthy that the decades in which famines occurred were ones in which population was static rather than falling.[1] In the 1920s and 1930s there were no famines, and the 1944 famine in Bengal was due to war conditions and transport difficulties rather than crop failure. However, the greater stability after 1920 may have been partly due to a lucky break in the weather cycle[2] rather than to a new stability of agriculture.

British rule reduced some of the old checks on Indian population growth. The main contribution was the ending of internal warfare and local banditry. There was some reduction in the incidence of famine. The death rate was also reduced to some degree by making ritual suicide and infanticide illegal. The British contributed to public health by introducing smallpox vaccination, establishing Western medicine and training modern doctors, by killing rats, and establishing quarantine procedures. As a result, the death rate fell and the population of India grew by 1947 to more than two-and-a-half times its size in 1757.

Industry
Several Indian authors have argued that British rule led to a de-industrialization of India. R. C. Dutt argued, 'India in the eighteenth century was a great manufacturing as well as a great agricultural country, and the products of the Indian loom supplied the markets of Asia and Europe. It is, unfortunately, true that the East India Company and the British Parliament, following the selfish commer-

Digby, *Prosperous British India*, London, 1901. More recently their assertion that the incidence of famine increased under British rule has been repeated in B. M. Bhatia, *Famines in India*, Asia Publishing House, Bombay, 1963, pp. 7–8: 'The frequency of famine showed a disconcerting increase in the nineteenth century.' However, there is no evidence to support this statement. In the period of British rule, the population started to increase which must have been due to some degree to a reduction in the impact of crop failure on mortality.

[1] See K. Davis, *op. cit.*, p. 28. In the 1870s Indian population was static, in the 1880s it rose 9 per cent, in the 1890s 1 per cent, in the first decade of the twentieth century 6 per cent, and in the second less than 1 per cent.

[2] See S. R. Sen, *Growth and Stability in Indian Agriculture*, Waltair, January 1967.

cial policy of a hundred years ago, discouraged Indian manufacturers in the early years of British rule in order to encourage the rising manufactures of England. Their fixed policy, pursued during the last decades of the eighteenth century and the first decades of the nineteenth, was to make India subservient to the industries of Great Britain, and to make the Indian people grow raw produce only, in order to supply material for the looms and manufactories of Great Britain.'[1]

R. Palme Dutt, writing forty years later, argued that the process had been continuous: 'the real picture of modern India is a picture of what has been aptly called "*de-industrialization*"—that is, the decline of the old handicraft industry without the compensating advance of modern industry. The advance of factory industry has not overtaken the decay of handicraft. The process of decay characteristic of the nineteenth century has been carried forward in the twentieth century and in the post-war period.'[2]

Nehru, in his popular history which is a conflation of the two Dutts, argued that the British deindustrialized India, and that this 'is the real the fundamental cause of the appalling poverty of the Indian people, and it is of comparatively recent origin'.[3]

There is a good deal of truth in the deindustrialization argument. Moghul India did have a bigger industry than any other country which became a European colony, and was unique in being an industrial exporter in pre-colonial times. A large part of the Moghul industry was destroyed in the course of British rule. However, it is important to understand precisely how this deindustrialization came about and to try to get some idea of its quantitative significance in different periods. Oversimplified explanations, which exaggerate the role of British commercial policy and ignore the role of changes in demand and technology, have been very common and have had some adverse impact on post-independence economic policy.[4]

Between 1757 and 1857 the British wiped out the Moghul court, and eliminated three-quarters of the warlord aristocracy (all except

[1] See R. C. Dutt, *op. cit.*, p. xxv (written in 1901).

[2] See R. P. Dutt, *India Today*, Gollancz, London, 1940, p. 165. Dutt based his conclusion in part on incomparable census material on industrial development. See D. and A. Thorner, *Land and Labour in India*, Asia Publishing House, New York, 1962, Chapter 6, for a refutation of the deindustrialization argument based on census figures.

[3] See J. Nehru, *The Discovery of India*, Day, New York, 1946, p. 299.

[4] D. R. Gadgil, *op. cit.*, is the only author who gives any stress to changes in demand patterns which were the indirect consequence (i.e. not induced by deliberate policy) of British rule.

those in princely states). They also eliminated more than half of the local chieftainry (zamindars) and in their place they established a bureaucracy with European tastes. The new rulers wore European clothes and shoes, drank imported beer, wines and spirits, and used European weapons. Their tastes were copied by the male members of the new Indian 'middle class' which arose to act as their clerks and intermediaries. As a result of these political and social changes, about three-quarters of the domestic demand for luxury handicrafts was destroyed. This was a shattering blow to manufacturers of fine muslins, jewellery, luxury clothing and footwear, decorative swords and weapons. It is not known how important these items were in national income, but my own guess would be that the home market for these goods was about 5 per cent of Moghul national income. The export market was probably another 1·5 per cent of national income, and most of this market was also lost. There was a reduction of European demand because of the change in sartorial tastes after the French revolution, and the greatly reduced price of more ordinary materials because of the revolution of textile technology in England.

The second blow to Indian industry came from massive imports of cheap textiles from England after the Napoleonic wars. In the period 1896–1913, imported piece goods supplied about 60 per cent of Indian cloth consumption,[1] and the proportion was probably higher for most of the nineteenth century. Home spinning, which was a spare-time activity of village women, was greatly reduced. A large proportion of village hand-loom weavers must have been displaced, though many switched to using factory instead of home-spun yarn. Even as late as 1940 a third of Indian piece goods were produced on hand looms.[2]

The new manufactured textile goods were considerably cheaper[3] and of better quality than hand-loom products, so their advent increased textile consumption. At the end of British rule, there can be no doubt that cloth consumption per head was substantially larger than in the Moghul period. We do not know how big an

[1] See A. I. Levkovsky, *Capitalism in India: Basic Trends in Its Development*, People's Publishing House, Bombay, 1966, p. 78.

[2] See R. C. Desai, *Standard of Living in India and Pakistan 1931–32 to 1940–41*, Popular Book Depot, Bombay, 1953, p. 95.

[3] See H. Heaton, *Economic History of Europe*, Harper and Row, London, 1965, p. 491: 'Between 1779 and 1812 the cost of making cotton yarn dropped nine-tenths. The mule's fine cheap yarn "brought to the masses of the people better goods than even the rich had been able to afford in the earlier period!" ' There was almost equal cost reduction in the weaving process. British textile exports rose thirtyfold in volume between the 1780s and the end of the Napeolonic wars; see P. Deane, *The First Industrial Revolution*, Cambridge University Press, 1965, p. 89.

increase in textile consumption occurred, but if *per capita* consumption of cotton cloth doubled (which seems quite plausible), then the displacement effect on hand-loom weavers would have been smaller than at first appears. The hand-loom weavers who produced a third of output in 1940 would have been producing two-thirds if there had been no increase in *per capita* consumption.

In time, India built up her own textile manufacturing industry which displaced British imports. But there was a gap of several decades before manufacturing started and a period of 130 years before British textile imports were eliminated. India could probably have copied Lancashire's technology more quickly if she had been allowed to impose a protective tariff in the way that was done in the U.S.A. and France in the first few decades of the nineteenth century, but the British imposed a policy of free trade. British imports entered India duty free, and when a small tariff was required for revenue purposes Lancashire pressure led to the imposition of a corresponding excise duty on Indian products to prevent them gaining a competitive advantage. This undoubtedly handicapped industrial development. If India had been politically independent, her tax structure would probably have been different. In the 1880s, Indian customs revenues were only 2·2 per cent of the trade turnover, i.e. the lowest ratio in any country. In Brazil, by contrast, import duties at that period were 21 per cent of trade turnover.[1] If India had enjoyed protection there is no doubt that its textile industry would have started earlier and grown faster.

The first textile mills were started in the 1850s by Indian capitalists who had made their money trading with the British and had acquired some education in English. Cotton textiles were launched in Bombay with financial and managerial help from British trading companies.

India was the first country in Asia to have a modern textile industry, preceding Japan by twenty years and China by forty years. Cotton mills were started in Bombay in 1851, and they concentrated on coarse yarns which were sold domestically and to China and Japan; yarn exports were about half of output.

Modern jute manufacturing started about the same time as cotton textiles. The first jute mill was built in 1854 and the industry expanded rapidly in the vicinity of Calcutta. The industry was largely in the hands of foreigners (mainly Scots). Between 1879 and 1913 the number of jute spindles rose tenfold—much faster than growth in the cotton textile industry. The jute industry was able to expand faster than cotton textiles because its sales did not depend so heavily

[1] See M. G. Mulhall, *The Dictionary of Statistics*, Routledge, London, 1899, pp. 172 and 258.

on the poverty-stricken domestic markets. Most of jute output was for export.

Coal mining, mainly in Bengal, was another industry which achieved significance. Its output, which by 1914 had reached 15·7 million tons, largely met the demands of the Indian railways.

In 1911 the first Indian steel mill was built by the Tata Company at Jamshedpur in Bihar. However, production did not take place on a significant scale before the First World War. The Indian steel industry started fifteen years later than in China, where the first steel mill was built at Hangyang in 1896. The first Japanese mill was built in 1898. In both China and Japan the first steel mills (and the first textile mills) were government enterpises.

Indian firms in industry, insurance and banking were given a boost from 1905 onwards by the *swadeshi* movement, which was a nationalist boycott of British goods in favour of Indian enterprise. During the First World War, lack of British imports strengthened the hold of Indian firms on the home market for textiles and steel. After the war, under nationalist pressure, the government started to favour Indian enterprise in its purchase of stores and it agreed to create a tariff commission in 1921 which started raising tariffs for protective reasons. By 1925, the average tariff level was 14 per cent[1] compared with 5 per cent pre-war. The procedure for fixing tariffs was lengthy and tariff protection was granted more readily to foreign-owned than to Indian firms,[2] but in the 1930s protection was sharply increased. The government was more willing to protect the textile industry when the threat came from Japan and not the U.K. Between 1930 and 1934 the tariff on cotton cloth was raised from 11 to 50 per cent, although British imports were accorded a margin of preference. As a result of these measures, there was considerable substitution of local textiles for imports. In 1896, Indian mills supplied only 8 per cent of total cloth consumption; in 1913, 20 per cent; in 1936, 62 per cent; and in 1945, 76 per cent.[3] By the latter date there were no imports of piece goods.

Until the end of the Napoleonic wars, cotton manufactures had been India's main export. They reached their peak in 1798, and in 1813 they still amounted to £2 million,[4] but thereafter they fell rapidly. Thirty years later, half of Indian imports were cotton

[1] See W. A. Lewis, *Economic Survey, 1919–39*, Allen and Unwin, London, 1949, p. 48.

[2] See M. Kidron, *Foreign Investments in India*, Oxford University Press, London, 1965, p. 13.

[3] See A. I. Levkovsky, *op. cit.*, pp. 78, 305, 335.

[4] See R. C. Dutt, *op. cit.*, p. 202.

textiles from Manchester. This collapse in India's main export caused a problem for the Company, which had to find ways to convert its rupee revenue into resources transferable to the U.K. The Company therefore promoted exports of raw materials on a larger scale, including sugar, silk, saltpetre and indigo, and greatly increased exports of opium which were traded against Chinese tea. These dope-peddling efforts provoked the Anglo-Chinese war of 1842, after which access to the Chinese market was greatly widened. By the middle of the nineteenth century opium was by far the biggest export of India, and remained in this position until the 1880s when its relative and absolute importance began to decline. Another new export was raw cotton, which could not compete very well in European markets against higher quality American and Egyptian cottons (except during the U.S. Civil War), but found a market in Japan and China. Sugar exports were built up after 1833 when the abolition of slavery raised West Indian production costs, but India had no long-run comparative advantage in sugar exports. Indigo (used to dye textiles) was an important export until the 1890s when it was hit by competition from German synthetic dyes. The jute industry boomed from the time of the Crimean War onwards, when the U.K. stopped importing flax from Russia. In addition to raw jute (shipped for manufacture in Dundee) India exported jute manufactures. Grain exports were also built up on a sizeable scale, mainly from the newly irrigated area of the Punjab. The tea industry was introduced to India from China and built up on a plantation basis. Tea exports became important from the 1860s onwards. Hides and skins and oil cake (used as animal feed and fertilizer) were also important raw material exports.

Manufactured textile exports from India began to increase in the 1850s when the first modern mills were established. The bulk of exports were yarn and crude piece goods which were sold in China and Japan. As the Chinese and Japanese were prevented by colonial-type treaties from imposing tariffs for manufactured imports they were wide open to Indian goods, and particularly cotton textiles and yarn. Indian jute manufactures were exported mainly to Europe and the U.S.A.

However, India began to suffer from Japanese competition in the 1890s. Indian yarn exports to Japan dropped sharply from 8,400 tons in 1890 to practically nothing in 1898, and India also suffered from Japanese competition in China. The Japanese set up factories in China after the Sino-Japanese War of 1894–5. Before this, India had supplied 96 per cent of Chinese yarn imports, the U.K. 4 per cent, and Japan none. Within three years the Japanese were supplying

Table III-1

Level of Asian Exports f.o.b. 1850–1950

(million dollars)

	1850	1913	1937	1950
Ceylon	5	76	124	328
China	24	294	516	(700)
India	89	786	717	1,178
Indonesia	24	270	550	800
Japan	1	354	1,207	820
Malaya	24	193	522	1,312
Philippines	n.a.	48	153	331
Thailand	3	43	76	304

N.B. Trade figures refer to customs area of the year concerned. In 1850 and 1913 the Indian area included Burma. The comparability of 1937 and 1950 figures is affected by the separation of Pakistan.

a quarter of Chinese imports, and by 1914 India was exporting less yarn to China than was Japan. During the First World War Japan made further progress in the Chinese market and by 1924 supplied three-quarters of Chinese imports. By 1928 India was exporting only 3 per cent of her yarn output.

By the end of the 1930s, Indian exports of yarn to China and Japan had disappeared, piece goods exports had fallen off, and India imported both yarn and piece goods from China and Japan.

Indian exports grew fairly rapidly in the period up to 1913, but their growth was slower than that of most other Asian countries which had a natural resource endowment offering greater opportunities for trade. As a consequence, in 1913, India had a smaller trade per head than most countries except China. Nevertheless, exports were 10·7 per cent of national income, probably a higher ratio than has been reached before or since.

Until 1898 India, like most Asian countries, was on the silver standard. In the 1870s the price of silver began to fall and the rupee depreciated against sterling. This led to some rise in the internal price level, but it helped to make Indian exports more competitive with those of the U.K., e.g. in the Chinese textile market. In 1898, India adopted a gold exchange standard which tied the rupee to sterling at a fixed value of 15 to 1. This weakened her competitiveness *vis-à-vis* China which remained on a depreciating silver standard, but its potential adverse effects were mitigated because Japan went on to the gold exchange standard at the same time.

During the First World War, when the sterling exchange rate was allowed to float, the rupee appreciated. Unfortunately, when sterling resumed a fixed (and overvalued) parity in 1925, the rupee exchange rate was fixed above the pre-war level. This overvaluation eased the fiscal problems of government in making transfers to the U.K. and enabled British residents in India, or those on Indian pensions in the U.K., to get more sterling for their rupees, but it made it necessary for domestic economic policy to be deflationary (in cutting wages) and greatly hindered Indian exports, particularly those to or competing with China and Japan.

As a result, Indian exports fell from 1913 to 1937, a poorer performance than that of almost any other country. At independence exports were less than 5 per cent of national income. If we look at Indian export performance from 1850 to 1950 it was worse than that of any other country in Asia (see Table III-1).

The Second World War gave a fillip to Indian industrial output, but there was not much increase in capacity because of the difficulty of importing capital goods and the lack of a domestic capital goods industry.

Many of the most lucrative commercial, financial, business and plantation jobs in the modern sector were occupied by foreigners. Although the East India Company's legally enforced monopoly privileges were ended in 1833, the British continued to exercise effective dominance through the system of 'managing agencies'. These agencies, originally set up by former employees of the East India Company, were used both to manage industrial enterprise and to handle most of India's international trade. They were closely linked with British banks, insurance and shipping companies. Managing agencies had a quasi-monopoly in access to capital,[1] and they had interlocking directorships which gave them control over supplies and markets. They dominated the foreign markets in Asia. They had better access to government officials than did Indians. The agencies were in many ways able to take decisions favourable to their own interests rather than those of shareholders. They were paid commissions based on gross profits or total sales and were often agents for the raw materials used by the companies they managed.

[1] In 1913, foreign banks held over three-quarters of total deposits, Indian Joint Stock Banks less than one-fourth. In the eighteenth century there had been very powerful Indian banking houses (dominated by the Jagath Seths) which handled revenue remittances and advances for the Moghul Empire, the Nawab of Bengal, the East India Company, other foreign companies, and Indian traders, and which also carried out arbitrage between Indian currency of different areas and vintages. These indigenous banking houses were largely pushed out by the British.

Thus the Indian capitalists who did emerge were highly dependent on British commercial capital and many sectors of industry were dominated by British firms, e.g. shipping, banking, insurance, coal, plantation crops and jute.

Indian industrial efficiency was hampered by the British administration's neglect of technical education, and the reluctance of British firms and managing agencies to provide training or managerial experience to Indians. Even in the Bombay textile industry, where most of the capital was Indian, 28 per cent of the managerial and supervisory staff were British in 1925 (42 per cent in 1895) and the British component was even bigger in more complex industries. This naturally raised Indian production costs.[1] At lower levels in the plant there was widespread use of jobbers for hiring workers and maintaining discipline, and workers themselves were a completely unskilled group who had to bribe the jobbers to get and retain their jobs. There were also problems of race, language and caste distinctions[2] between management, supervisors and workers. The small size and very diversified output of the enterprises hindered efficiency. It is partly for these reasons (and the overvaluation of the currency) that Indian exports had difficulty in competing with Japan.

The basic limitations on the growth of industrial output were the extreme poverty of the rural population, and the fact that a large proportion of the elite had a taste for imported goods or exported their purchasing power. The government eventually provided tariff protection but did not itself create industrial plants, sponsor development banks, or give preference to local industry in allotting contracts. The banking system gave little help to industry and technical education was poor. Most of these things changed when India became independent except the first and most important, i.e. the extreme poverty of the rural population which limited the expansion of the market for industrial goods.

By the time of independence, large-scale factory industry in India employed less than 3 million people as compared with $12\frac{1}{4}$ million

[1] See D. H. Buchanan, *The Development of Capitalist Enterprise in India*, Cass, London, 1966, pp. 211 and 321, who gives figures of the cost of European managerial personnel. In the Tata steelworks in 1921–2 the average salary of foreign supervisory staff was 13,527 rupees a year, whereas Indian workers got 240 rupees. These foreigners cost twice as much as in the U.S.A. and were usually less efficient. Use of foreign staff often led to inappropriate design, e.g. multistorey mills in a hot climate or use of mule instead of ring spindles.

[2] M. D. Morris has suggested that caste was not an obstacle to industrial development, because the industrial labour power included workers of all castes. See M. D. Morris, *The Emergence of an Industrial Labour Force in India*, Cambridge University Press, 1965.

in small-scale industry and handicrafts, and a labour force of 160 million.[1] This may appear meagre, but India's *per capita* industrial output at independence was higher than elsewhere in Asia outside Japan, and more than half of India's exports were manufactures. British policy was less repressive to local industry than that of other colonial powers, and had permitted the emergence of a small but powerful class of Indian entrepreneurs. It should be noted, however, that modern industry was heavily concentrated in Calcutta, Bombay and Ahmedabad. The area which was to become Pakistan had practically no industry at all.

Table III-2

Industrial Growth in the Last Half Century of British Rule

	Small-scale enterprise		Factory establishments	
	Employment (thousands)	Value added (million 1938 Rs.)	Employment (thousands)	Value added (million 1938 Rs.)
Average of 1900 and 1901	13,308	2,296	601	379
Average of 1945 and 1946	12,074	2,083	2,983	2,461

Source: S. Sivasubramonian, *op. cit.*, for employment and value added in factories. For small-scale enterprise I assume value added to move proportionately to employment.

In the last half century of British rule the output of factory industry rose about sixfold (about 4·2 per cent a year) whereas the output of small-scale industry declined. Their joint output rose about two-thirds (1·2 per cent a year), and per head of population, joint output was rising by 0·4 per cent a year. We know that output in the modern factory sector was zero in 1850, and if we assume that small enterprise output grew parallel with population from 1850 to 1900, then total industrial output would have grown by 0·8 per cent a year in this period, or about 0·3 per cent a year per head of population. Some increase seems plausible in this period of railway development and expanding international trade. It therefore seems possible that in the last century of British rule, *per capita* output of industrial goods rose by a third. But in the first century of British rule, i.e. 1757–1857, it seems certain that industrial output fell per head of population because (*a*) the home and domestic market for luxury

[1] See S. Sivasubramonian, *op. cit.*

goods was cut so drastically; (b) the home market for yarn and cheap cloth was invaded by foreign competition. Over the whole period of British rule it therefore seems likely that industrial output per head of the population was not significantly changed.

The Economic Burden of Foreign Rule

The major burden of foreign rule arose from the fact that the British raj was a regime of expatriates. Under an Indian administration, income from government service would have accrued to the local inhabitants and not to foreigners. The diversion of upper-class income into the hands of foreigners inhibited the development of local industry because it put purchasing power into the hands of people with a taste for foreign goods. This increased imports and was particularly damaging to the luxury handicraft industries.

Another important effect of foreign rule on the long-run growth potential of the economy was the fact that a large part of its potential savings were siphoned abroad. This 'drain' of funds from India to the U.K. has been a point of major controversy between Indian nationalist historians and defenders of the British raj. However, the only real grounds for controversy are statistical. There can be no denial that there was a substantial outflow which lasted for 190 years. If these funds had been invested in India they could have made a significant contribution to raising income levels.

The first generation of British rulers was rapacious. Clive took quarter of a million pounds for himself as well as a jagir worth £27,000 a year, but the British did not pillage on the scale of Nadir Shah, who probably took as much from India in one year as the East India Company did in the twenty years following the battle of Plassey.[1] They were also shrewd enough to realize that it was not in their long-run interest to devastate the country.

However, British salaries were high: the Viceroy received £25,000 a year, and governors £10,000. The starting salary in the engineering service was £420 a year or about sixty times the average income of the Indian labour force. From 1757 to 1919, India also had to meet

---

[1] There is a tendency amongst Marxist and anti-British historians to exaggerate the size of the Indian plunder. R. P. Dutt argues that 'the spoliation of India was the hidden source of accumulation which played an all important role in helping to make possible the Industrial Revolution in England', see R. P. Dutt, *op. cit.* An even more extreme view is taken by P. A. Baran, *The Political Economy of Growth*, Prometheus, New York, 1957, p. 145. See also B. Adams, *The Law of Civilization and Decay*, New York, 1910, and W. Digby, *Prosperous British India*, 1901. In fact a good deal of the Indian revenue was used to finance local wars and did not reach the U.K. The latest scholarly estimates suggest that the transfer to the U.K. was about one-tenth of the amounts estimated by Digby.

administrative expenses in London, first of the East India Company, and then of the India Office, as well as other minor but irritatingly extraneous charges. The cost of British staff was raised by long home leave in the U.K., early retirement and lavish amenities in the form of subsidized housing, utilities, rest houses, etc.

Under the rule of the East India Company, official transfers to the U.K. rose gradually until they reached about £3·5 million in 1856, the year before the mutiny. In addition, there were private remittances. In the twenty years 1835–54, India's average annual balance on trade and bullion was favourable by about £4·5 million a year.

During the period of direct British rule from 1858 to 1947, official transfers of funds to the U.K. by the colonial government were called the 'Home Charges'. They mainly represented debt service, pensions, India Office expenses in the U.K., purchases of military items and railway equipment. Government procurement of civilian goods, armaments and shipping was carried out almost exclusively in the U.K. By the 1930s these home charges were in the range of £40 to £50 million a year. Some of these flows would have occurred in a non-colonial economy, e.g. debt service on loans used to finance railway development, but a large part of the debt was incurred as a result of colonial wars. Some government expenditure was on imports which an independent government would have bought from local manufacturers. Of these official payments, we can legitimately consider service charges on non-productive debt, pensions and furlough payments as a balance of payment drain due to colonialism.

There were also substantial private remittances by British officials in India either as savings or to meet educational and other family charges in the U.K. In the inter-war period, these amounted to about £10 million a year, and Naoroji estimated that they were running at the same level in 1887.[1] These items were clearly the result of colonial rule. In addition, there were dividend and interest remittances by shipping and banking interests, plantations, and other British investors; to some extent, these were normal commercial transactions, but there was a large element of monopoly profit due to the privileged position of British business in India; and, in many cases, the original assets were not acquired by remitting funds to India but by savings

[1] See A. K. Banerji, *India's Balance of Payments*, Asia Publishing House, Bombay, 1963, p. 136; D. Naoroji, *Poverty and Un-British Rule in India*, London, 1901 (Government of India Reprint), Delhi, 1962, p. 223; C. Lewis, *America's Stake in International Investments*, Brookings, Washington, D.C., 1938, p. 462, suggests that the annual remittances including business profits from India and China were already 6 million in 1838. The bulk of this would be from India as at that time there were probably less than 250 British residing in China, see C. Lewis, *op. cit.*, p. 176.

from income earned locally, or by purchase of property on favourable terms, e.g. the land acquisitions of plantation companies. About a third of the private profit remittances should therefore be treated as the profits of colonialism.

Table III-3

India's Balance on Merchandise and Bullion, 1835–1967

	Balance in current prices (annual average)	Balance in 1948–9 prices (£ million)	Per capita balance at 1948–9 prices (£)
1835–54	4·5	n.a.	n.a.
1855–74	7·3	50·0	0·21
1875–94	13·4	80·0	0·30
1895–1913	16·8	77·6	0·26
1914–34	22·5	59·2	0·19
1935–46	27·9	66·1	0·17
1948–57 (India and Pakistan)	−99·9	−97·6	−0·21
1958–67 (India and Pakistan)	−472·7	−384·7	−0·67

Note: This table understates the Indian surplus (and overstates the deficit) because imports are recorded c.i.f. and exports f.o.b. Constant price figures derived by using national income deflator.

Source: Trade figures deflated by the national income deflator and in the colonial period by the price index of M. Mukherjee, *National Income of India*, Statistical Publishing Society, Calcutta, 1969.

The total 'drain' due to government pensions and leave payments, interest on non-railway official debt, private remittances for education and savings, and a third of commercial profits amounted to about 1·5 per cent of national income of undivided India from 1921 to 1938[1] and was probably a little larger before that. Net investment was about 5 per cent of national income at the end of British rule, so about a quarter of Indian savings were transferred out of the economy, and foreign exchange was lost which could have paid for imports of capital goods. As a consequence of this foreign drain the Indian balance of trade and bullion[2] was always positive as can be

[1] 'Drain' estimate derived from A. K. Banerji, *op. cit.*, and national income figures from Appendix B.
[2] India continued to be a massive net importer of bullion under British rule.

seen in Table III-3. If we take Table III-2 as a rough indicator of the movement in the colonial burden (though not of its absolute level) it would seem that it was biggest around the 1880s. Since independence the picture has been completely reversed and there is now a substantial inflow of resources because of foreign aid.

In spite of its constant favourable balance of trade, India acquired substantial debts. By 1939 foreign assets in India amounted to $2·8 billion, of which about $1·5 billion was government bonded debt and the rest represented direct investment (mainly tea, other plantations and the jute industry).

India did not reduce its foreign debt during the First World War as many other developing countries did. Instead, there were two 'voluntary' war gifts to the U.K. amounting to £150 million ($730 million). India also contributed one-and-a-quarter million troops, which were financed from the Indian budget. The 'drain' of funds to England continued in the interwar years because of home charges and profit remittances. There was also a small outflow of British capital.

In the depression of 1929–33, many developing countries defaulted on foreign debt or froze dividend transfers, but this was not possible for India. The currency was kept at par with sterling and devalued in 1931, but the decisions were based on British rather than Indian needs. Furthermore, the salaries of civil servants remained at high levels,[1] and the burden of official transfers increased in a period of falling prices.

During the Second World War, India's international financial position was transformed. The U.K. had enormous military expenditures for its own troops in India and also financed local costs of allied troops under Lease-Lend arrangements. Indian war finance was much more inflationary than in the U.K. and prices rose threefold, so these local costs of troop support were extremely high in terms of sterling, as the exchange rate remained unchanged. As a result, India was able to liquidate $1·2 billion of pre-war debt and acquired reserve assets of $5·1 billion, ending the war a large net creditor.[2] These new assets and the disappearance of the colonial drain gave a formidable boost to post-war development policy.

---

[1] There was a cut in civil service salaries in 1931, but it applied only to new recruits.

[2] In 1939, India had a foreign debt of 4,485 million rupees and assets of 739 million. In 1945 its official debt was only 175 million and its assets 17,243 million rupees. See K. C. Chacko, *The Monetary and Fiscal Policy of India*, Vora, Bombay, 1957.

Conclusions

There has been a good deal of controversy amongst statisticians about the rate of growth of income in India in the colonial period. The argument is politically coloured and the statistics are poor. For the last fifty years of British rule there is enough statistical information to make rough estimates of the growth of national income. My own estimates, which are based largely on work by Blyn and Sivasubramonian, show no increase in *per capita* income over the years 1900–46 (see Appendix B). Other observers have estimates which show some growth over this period as well as in the period from 1857.[1] Although I think my estimates are the best available, I have enough scepticism about the basic agricultural data to believe that the other estimates could be right for the wrong reasons and that there may have been some rise in *per capita* income from 1857 to 1947. There are no estimates for the movement in income from Clive's conquest to the Mutiny, but there could not have been much net progress in real income per head before the development of railways, modern industry, irrigation and the big expansion in international trade, and there are reasons for thinking that there was some decline.[2] From the beginning of British conquest in 1757 to independence, it seems unlikely that *per capita* income could have increased by more than a third and it probably did not increase at all. In the U.K. itself there was a tenfold increase in *per capita* income over these two centuries.[3] The most noticeable change in the economy was the rise in population from about 170 million to 420 million from 1757 to 1947.

However, there were some significant changes in social structure and in the pattern of output. The social pyramid was truncated because the British lopped off most of the top three layers of the Moghul hierarchy, i.e. the Moghul court, the Moghul aristocracy and quasi-autonomous princes (a quarter of these survived), and the local chieftainry (zamindars who survived in about 40 per cent of India). In place of these people the British installed a modern

[1] See M. Mukherjee, *National Income of India*, *op. cit.*, p. 61, who shows a 50 per cent rise from 1857 to 1945 (including a 28 per cent rise from 1900 to 1945). S. Sivasubramonian, *op. cit.*, shows a 23 per cent growth in *per capita* income from 1900 to 1946, but in several important cases his deflation procedures seem inadequate. See Appendix B.

[2] This the view of T. Raychaudhuri, *The Indian Economic and Social History Review*, March 1968. M. D. Morris expresses a contrary view in the same journal.

[3] See P. Deane and W. A. Cole, *op. cit.*, pp. 68, 282, 329–30, and A. Maddison, *Economic Growth in Japan and the U.S.S.R.*, Allen and Unwin, London, 1969, p. 159.

bureaucracy which took a smaller share of national income. The newcomers had a more modest life-style than the Moghuls, but siphoned a large part of their savings out of the country and provided almost no market for India's luxury handicrafts. The modern factory sector which they created produced only 7·5 per cent of national income at the end of British rule and thus did little more than replace the old luxury handicrafts and part of the village textile production.

The British reduced the tax squeeze on agriculture and turned warlords into landlords, but the new order had little dynamism. A good deal of the old fuzziness about property rights remained, and landlords were still largely parasitic. The bigger zamindars copied the Moghul life-style by maintaining hordes of retainers and huge mansions, the smaller landowner's ambition was to stop working and enhance his ritual purity by establishing a seedy gentility. Very little incentive was provided for investment and almost nothing was done to promote technical change in agriculture. At the bottom of society the position of sharecropping tenantry and landless labourers remained wretched. In urban areas a new Westernized 'middle class' of Indians emerged and became the major challenge to the British raj.

Table III-4 gives a rough idea of the social structure around 1938. Some of the figures are based on detective work and hunches and should be regarded as well-informed guesses rather than firm estimates. However, the table illustrates the orders of magnitude involved and, as these are often misunderstood, there is some justification for tabulating them.[1] It can be seen that the British were a very thin layer at the top of society but they took about 5 per cent of national income. Their allies, the native princes and zamindars, took about 3 per cent. Eight per cent is a sizeable proportion for the ruling class but, under the Moghul regime, the equivalent group collected 15 per cent of national income in taxes and spent most of it on their own consumption.

Immediately under this group were two new indigenous classes—capitalists and professionals—who became the dominant elite in independent India. They were relatively larger in number and probably had a bigger share of national income than their counterparts under the Moghuls, i.e. the *shroffs* (indigenous urban bankers), merchants, *qazis* and *pandits* (lawyers), *hakims* (indigenous doctors), etc.

There were also changes in the lower class in the non-village

[1] For village society I have derived estimates of income and social class from Tables VI-1 and VI-2, assuming that they were about the same at the end of the colonial period. Other estimates are from miscellaneous budgetary and census material, and national income data.

Table III-4

Social Structure at the End of British Rule

Percentage of labour force		Percentage of national income
18	NON-VILLAGE ECONOMY	44
0·06	British officials and military British capitalists, plantation owners, traders, bankers and managers	5
	Native princes Big zamindars and jagirdars	3
0·94	Indian capitalists, merchants and managers	3
	The new Indian professional class	3
17	Petty traders, small entrepreneurs, traditional professions, clerical and manual workers in government, soldiers, railway workers, industrial workers, urban artisans, servants, sweepers and scavengers	30
75	VILLAGE ECONOMY	54
9	Village rentiers, rural moneylenders, small zamindars, tenants-in-chief	20
20	Working proprietors, protected tenants	18
29	Tenants-at-will, sharecroppers, village artisans and servants	12
17	Landless labourers, scavengers	4
7	TRIBAL ECONOMY	2

economy. At the end of British rule there were 3 million factory workers making cheap textiles and jute sacking, whose Moghul predecessors had worked on muslins and silks, and a million railway workers who had no earlier counterpart. This lower-class urban group was probably bigger than in Moghul times, because they had displaced some of the village artisans.

Within village society the social structure was probably similar to that in Moghul India, with the two top economic groups corresponding to the old dominant castes, the next group to peasant castes, and the bottom group consisting largely of untouchables. The main difference from the Moghul economy is that village proprietors and tenants-in-chief were no longer heavily squeezed by taxation and their share of national income had probably increased.

Thus the main gainers from the British regime (apart from the British) were the so-called 'middle' class of Indian capitalists and professionals, and the village squirearchy. Most of these were high caste Hindus though the Parsis and Sikhs did fairly well. The main losers were the Muslims who had formed the major part of the Moghul aristocracy, officer corps, lawyers, and artisans in the luxury handicrafts.

Chapter IV

The Social Origins and Ideology of the Nationalist Movement

In most countries which have been colonies of economically-advanced powers, nationalism has been more intense and complicated than it has ever been in Europe. In India, as elsewhere, there are four main types of nationalism which are worth distinguishing, because they have had different effects on social and economic policy since independence.

The first kind of nationalism was simply *status quo* conservatism. This had little lasting appeal because it had no ideology, offered nothing to compete with the promise of Western civilization, was led by social forces which had already suffered a first defeat, and did not present a real challenge to the colonial power. The Indian Mutiny of 1857 falls into this category.

The second type of movement was bourgeois (step-in-your-shoes) nationalism. Nationalists of this kind (like D. Naoroji and R. C. Dutt) accepted Western values and many of the changes in the social system brought about by colonialism. They wished to widen the area of the economy in which modern capitalism operated, and were willing to use weapons such as protective tariffs to this end which the colonial power did not use (because of its interest in preserving markets for the metropolitan country). The major instrument of modernization at their disposal after independence was the state apparatus and bureaucracy left by colonialism. This kind of nationalism was in gestation amongst Hindus in India from the 1820s onwards and was *the* prime brand of organized nationalism from 1885 to 1905.

After 1905, a new kind of populist (indigenist revivalist) national-ism emerged which attempted to gain popular support by more explicit denunciation of colonial rule. It stressed the value of indigenous institutions which the colonial power was alleged to be destroying. The leaders of the movement did not simply want a return to the *ancien régime* as did the *status quo* nationalists. They wanted to revive old institutions in a purified form—often different enough from reality to be almost mythological. The leaders of this brand of nationalism were in a delicate position because many of them were basically bourgeois (step-in-your-shoes) nationalists using new symbols as a tactic to arouse popular support from the illiterate masses. The tactic was made necessary because the colonial regime was not willing to bow out to polite requests. Not all populist leaders were cynics, the most successful ones were usually fervent believers. Indigenist revivalism provided psychological strength and self-respect which was particularly needed in India because of (a) the element of racist arrogance on the part of the colonial regime; (b) the fact that Hindus had experienced a double colonial yoke, i.e. the Moghuls and the British. Furthermore, the religion of Hindus was specific to India, so there was a closer association between religion and nationalism than in countries where religion is a more oecumenic force. The intensity of this indigenist feeling explains the emergence of Gandhi as a saint-politician and his dominance from the 1920s onwards. It also explains a good deal about Indian economic and social policy since independence, with its emphasis on the village as a community, the virtues of hand-loom weaving, the holy attributes of self-sufficiency.[1]

The fourth brand of nationalism was social-revolutionary. Social revolutionaries recognized the virtue of Western civilization, and regarded most of traditional society as an encumbrance to progress. They were therefore willing to break up the old society and experiment with new social and economic forms. In India, most social revolutionaries were socialists or communists, but this is not necessarily the case, e.g. it was not true of Mustapha Kemal in Turkey, or of many Mexican nationalists. In India, this last form of nationalism was extremely weak because (a) traditional institutions such as caste have such strong religious sanctions; (b) the social structure is not as sharply polarized as in most countries, so that many more people have a stake in the *status quo*. The real weakness of the social revolutionary element in India was disguised by the political and intellectual eminence of Nehru, who was a social-revolutionary in theory and only to a limited extent in practice. Nehru's leadership position is testimony to the traditional Indian tolerance for ambiguity and amorphous organizations. He could not have achieved leadership without very substantial compromise with other forms of nationalism. In interpreting economic and social policy in post-independence India, it is therefore useful to remember

[1] Indigenism is a powerful force in many countries. Sometimes its content remains rather vague, such as in 'African socialism', but in Mexico there is a very specific attachment to the *ejido* as a collective form of farm property. The Russian Narodniks of the nineteenth century, with their emphasis on the virtues of the *mir* as a form of collective property, were the precursors of modern indigensim.

that it incorporates three types of ideology, i.e. bourgeois (step-in-your-shoes) nationalism, indigenist revivalism, and a much milder dose of social revolution than is generally assumed.

The origins of Pakistani nationalism are simpler than those in India. The Muslims were the main losers from British rule because it completely changed their social status in the eyes of Hindus. Previously they had been the ruling class, now they were merely a religious minority, sometimes considered to have lower status than outcastes. A feeling of resentment and despair had grown steadily amongst Muslims since the death of Aurangzeb. Muslim rulers had experienced defeat at the hands of the Hindus, Sikhs and British. Their cultural life received a crushing blow in 1857 when the Moghul court was destroyed. This induced a feeling of almost total anomie, and there was a steady reversion to Islamic fundamentalism. Hindu-Persian associations which Islam had acquired during the Moghul period were cast aside, and there was a revival of the puritanical doctrines of the early Caliphate and a stress on the oecumenic links of Muslims with Islam as a whole.

Acceptance of Western civilization took fifty years longer for Muslims than it did for Hindus.[1] After this, Muslims took part in the general nationalist movement in its bourgeois (step-in-your-shoes) phase. In 1906, the Muslim League was founded as a separate political party. At first the Muslim League was more of an anti-nationalist than a nationalist movement. Its leaders were people like the Agha Khan and the Nawab of Comilla, allies of the British who feared the consequences of independence for their own social class. But their movement was also a reaction to the first important manifestation of indigenist nationalism. In the campaign against Lord Curzon's partition of Bengal, the nationalist movement attracted popular support by using Hindu religious symbols, and this naturally alarmed Muslims.[2] The 1905 movement was important because it was ultimately successful, and in 1911 the British reversed Curzon's

[1] The great Hindu protagonist of Western values was Ram Mohan Roy (1774–1833) of Bengal, who became a correspondent of Jeremy Bentham and is buried in Bristol. In 1828 he founded a movement to rationalize Hinduism (later known as Brahmo Samaj). He denounced polytheism and idolatry, tried to improve the status of women and to mitigate the rigours of caste. He welcomed the use of English as a medium of instruction and was as contemptuous of Sanskrit education as Macaulay. His Muslim counterpart was Sayyid Ahmad Khan who realized the adverse economic consequences of Muslim quietism, urged the Muslims to co-operate loyally with the British and founded the Aligarh Anglo-Oriental College in 1875 in which instruction was given in English, and which later became the Muslim university.

[2] Apart from the religious elements in the campaign propaganda, there was some real difference of interest between the communities. East Bengal was a

partition. The most powerful weapon used by the nationalists was the boycott of British imports and a campaign in favour of Indian goods (swadeshi). Sales and imports of British textiles, matches, soap, biscuits, cigarettes, toys and liquor all suffered badly. This caused real damage to British interests and won the nationalists the adherence and financial support of the Indian business community who profited substantially from this action.

The indigenist element in Indian nationalism became stronger in 1920 when Gandhi took over the leadership of Congress.[1] His extreme degree of indigenism antagonized some of the bourgeois nationalists, who split away from Congress to form the Liberal Party, and it led M. A. Jinnah, the most prominent Muslim amongst the bourgeois nationalists, to break with Congress. Eventually, after a great deal of hesitation, Jinnah embraced the idea of partitioning India, and turned the Muslim League into a mass party in 1940. However, the Muslim League was not a religious movement. The motivation was essentially bourgeois nationalism, its religious content was as much anti-Hindu as pro-Islamic.

This is a very important quality of Pakistani nationalism which helps to explain social and economic policy since independence. The political system of Pakistan which Jinnah created was Viceregal, and the primary locus of power has been the bureaucratic military elite. It is not a copy of Whitehall democracy but of the British colonial apparatus. It is not a theocratic state but bourgeois nationalism in its purest form, undiluted with indigenist mysticism, or social revolutionary intent.

The Pakistan movement never had any content of social reform. This was partly because some of the deepest social problems of India, such as casteism, arise from Hindu and not Muslim institu-

---

predominantly Muslim province which offered Muslims new job opportunities in its new capital of Dacca. The losers were Hindus who dominated in Calcutta.

[1] Gandhi was not an orthodox Hindu but an eclectic disciple of Ruskin and Tolstoy, who issued simple moral imperatives, some of which were intended to reform Hinduism. He gave up Western clothing for a hand-woven loincloth. He lived in an *ashram* (hermitage) surrounded by disciples. He gave up sexual relations with his wife, and lived on a diet of goat's milk and dates. He rejected not only the British raj, but Western civilization. In the long run he thought India could do without lawyers, railways, motor cars, telegraphs, hospitals, doctors, modern medicine or imports. People could lead purer lives by limiting their wants. He glorified the virtues of the Indian village community, which, in his mythology, was a place of idyllic harmony. He regarded landlords and industrialists as trustees, urged them to be charitable, and did not agitate against the autocratic rule of the Indian princes. However, he did support improved status for women and urged better treatment of untouchables, whom he dubbed as *harijans* (children of God).

tions. Furthermore, the Muslims did not need the mythology of an idyllic village society to bolster their self-respect—they had been rulers of India for 700 years before the British came. Jinnah was not an austere holy man in a loincloth, but a sybaritic lawyer who wore Savile Row suits, so the khadi movement had little appeal to him. Finally, Jinnah and his supporters were men of property who did not wish to change the social order but simply wanted to ensure that their community got a fair share of the pickings. In fact Jinnah gave the social problem no real consideration. He was not even conscious of the irony when he said once in London, 'Democracy is the blood of Mussalmans . . . I give you an example. Very often, when I go to a mosque, my chauffeur stands side by side with me. Mussalmans believe in fraternity, equality and liberty.'[1]

[1] See H. Bolitho, *Jinnah, Creator of Pakistan*, Murray, London, 1964, p. 173.

Chapter V

Reasons for the Acceleration of Economic Growth since Independence

India

In the years since independence, Indian economic growth has been much faster than in the colonial period. From 1948 to 1969 real national income rose by 3·3 per cent per year.[1] For pre-war years, there are crop statistics back into the 1890s, so that it is possible to make rough but acceptable estimates for 1900–46.[2] These show a compound growth rate of real national income amounting to 0·7 per cent a year in the last half century of colonial rule. Population growth was 0·8 per cent a year from 1900 to 1946 and rose to 2·4 per cent a year in 1948–69. Therefore *per capita* income has grown by 0·9 per cent a year since independence, compared with a more or less stagnant level from 1900 to 1946.

There are five reasons why economic growth has accelerated since independence:

(*a*) With the departure of the colonial administration the emphasis of bureaucratic action has been switched from law and order to development, and bigger taxes have been levied to pay for the expansion of government services. From 1950 to 1969, government current expenditure on development rose from 2·2 per cent to 6·5 per cent of national income, and the proportion of the labour force working in administration doubled. The biggest expansion has been in areas related to production. In rural areas there are now 80,000 government employees doing various kinds of extension work, whereas in British times there were only about 2,000. In the field of research and development there are now 62,000 scientists and technicians in government employ. Universities and technical schools have greatly increased in number. There are several new ministries—for Industrial Development, Irrigation and Power, Petroleum and Chemicals, Mines and Metals, Steel and Heavy Engineering, and a Department of Atomic Energy. Stronger policy weapons are used to

---

[1] This figure is based on the official estimates presented in Ministry of Finance, *Economic Survey*, Delhi, 1970, 1948–60 at 1948 prices, is based on the 'conventional' series, and 1960–8 on the 'revised' series. For 1969 it was assumed that real national income rose by 5·25 per cent, as indicated in the Fourth Plan.

[2] See Appendix B for the estimates for 1900–46.

favour domestic industry. Tariffs are substantially higher and greatly reinforced by quantitative restrictions. The government itself has entered industry on a large scale. Private industry has received help from new development banks, agriculture has benefited from a vast expansion of government-sponsored co-operative credit.

(b) The rate of investment has been raised from about 5 per cent to about 11 per cent of national income in 1967. Government investment is now about 6 per cent of national income, compared with about 2 per cent at most in colonial times.[1] In the old days, government investment was limited largely to canals and railways. Now the commitment to infrastructure in irrigation, transport and power is bigger, and government enterprises produce about 10 per cent of the output of factory industry. Private investment has risen from 3 to 5 per cent of national income. Part of the increase in investment has been financed by an increase in taxes, some by changes in private savings. The protection and subsidies given to industry have put extra money into the pockets of relatively rich people with a high propensity to save. The tax structure, particularly in the corporate sector, encourages saving and investment rather than consumption. Restrictions on imports of luxury goods and the deposition of princes and zamindars has changed the social ethos away from conspicuous consumption towards greater austerity. Gold hoards and palaces are less important. The fact that many farmers have better titles to land has encouraged them to invest. Finally, better technological opportunities, and the obvious government push for growth, have strengthened private investment incentives.

(c) The increase in investment was financed partly by an increased domestic effort, but half of the increase has been financed by the change in foreign trade and aid. Before the war the colonial 'drain' siphoned funds out of the country and there was a trade surplus. Since independence there has been a trade deficit. There were large exchange reserves to draw upon until 1958, and a considerable amount of foreign aid thereafter. The pre-war drain amounted to 1·5 per cent of national income, but from 1950 to 1965 the inflow of foreign resources represented more than 2 per cent, i.e. a swing in India's favour since colonial times of 3·5 per cent of national income.

(d) The accelerated growth in output is due in part to faster population growth. Before the war, population grew at 0·8 per cent a year, but has now risen to about 2·4 per cent. The acceleration occurred because of the decline in mortality. Life expectation rose

[1] See M. J. T. Thavaraj, 'Rate of Public Investment in India, 1898–1938', in T. Raychaudhuri (ed.), *Contributions to Indian Economic History*, Mukhopadhyay, Calcutta, 1963.

from thirty to fifty. As a result the labour force has grown more than twice as fast as in pre-war years and there have been improvements in health and education which raised its quality. It may well be that there has been some increase in the degree of unemployment or idle labour time, but there is no real evidence on this point and we can certainly not assume that the increase in the labour supply has simply increased unemployment. There is no doubt that welfare would have been substantially higher if it had been possible to cut birth rates to match the fall in mortality. There would have been fewer workers but they would have had higher productivity because the capital stock would have been spread less thinly. However, we must not forget that increased labour supply contributes something to the growth of output even in Indian conditions.

(e) Finally, growth has accelerated because technological opportunities are greater now than in pre-war years. The pace of technological innovation has speeded up in the world as a whole with the world-wide acceleration in economic growth. Ideas are communicated more rapidly and easily now that businessmen, technicians and government officials can move quickly by air instead of wasting weeks on a sea journey. Government spends more now on research and technological transfer than it did in pre-war years, and the higher rate of capital formation means that new technology can be more readily embodied in the production process. Some of the most spectacular improvements have been in fields which require little capital, such as antibiotics or D.D.T. which have cut mortality, or the new seeds which have substantially increased farm income. Foreign trade is now heavily concentrated on capital goods and is a major instrument of technological diffusion.

Although India's post-war growth is much better than it was under colonial rule, and is a legitimate source of national pride, we must also remember that acceleration in growth is a world-wide phenomenon. It has happened to almost every country. To judge the effectiveness of policy we must therefore make international as well as historical comparisons. In fact, India's post-war performance is well below the average for developing countries (though not as much below as it was in pre-war years).[1] This suggests that Indian growth strategy may have been less effective than that of other countries. But before jumping to this conclusion we must see whether India's growth *potential* was lower than that elsewhere. There are, in fact, several reasons why this might have been the case:

[1] See A. Maddison, *Economic Progress and Policy in Developing Countries*, Allen and Unwin, London, 1970.

(*a*) Its absolute level of income is extremely low, even by Asian standards. In Table V-1, which gives comparative figures for a sample of twenty-two countries, India occupies the twenty-first position. There may be some 'advantages of backwardness', but it seems likely that the lower the income of a country the more difficult it may be to raise domestic funds for development, either by taxation or by private savings.

(*b*) India's foreign capital receipts have been large in absolute terms, but on a *per capita* basis they have been well below the average for developing countries. In our sample of twenty-two countries, India occupies the twentieth position (see Table V-2). The size of foreign aid and private capital receipts is not wholly independent of India's economic policy, but India is so big that it has a size factor working against large *per capita* receipts of foreign capital, particularly in the form of aid. It therefore seems permissible to regard the low level of foreign capital as a quasi-exogenous unfavourable growth factor.

(*c*) India has poor natural resources. By comparison with Latin America or Africa there is heavy pressure of population on the land. However, this is not a very convincing argument in the Asian context because there are other countries like Japan, Taiwan or Korea which have smaller resources but fast growth rates. The chief natural disadvantage is perhaps the uncertainty of the climate. In 1965 and 1966 there was a colossal drought, and farm output fell by 12 per

Table V-1

Levels of Real Income *Per Capita* in 1965

($ at U.S. relative prices)

Argentina	1,272	Mexico	423
Brazil	482	Pakistan	152
Ceylon	271	Peru	397
Chile	863	Philippines	269
Colombia	375	South Korea	255
Egypt	295	Spain	975
Ghana	230	Taiwan	573
Greece	676	Thailand	254
India	182	Turkey	289
Israel	1,340	Venezuela	1,264
Malaya	528	Yugoslavia	736

Source: A. Maddison, *Economic Progress and Policy in Developing Countries*, Allen and Unwin, London, 1970, p. 295.

Table V-2

Per Capita Net Receipts of Foreign Capital 1960–5

(annual average in U.S. dollars)

Argentine	9·7	Mexico	8·2
Brazil	4·4	Pakistan	4·2
Ceylon	2·0	Peru	8·2
Chile	22·9	Philippines	4·8
Colombia	8·4	South Korea	10·4
Egypt	10·1	Spain	15·4
Ghana	10·7	Taiwan	8·6
Greece	37·7	Thailand	4·1
India	2·2	Turkey	7·3
Israel	212·4	Venezuela	−24·9
Malaya	3·2	Yugoslavia	11·6

Source: A. Maddison, *op. cit.*, pp. 219 and 240.

Table V-3

Land Availability Per Person Employed in Agriculture in 1965)

(hectares per person)

Argentine	91·6	Mexico	14·8
Brazil	11·0	Pakistan	0·9
Ceylon	0·8	Peru	18·8
Chile	21·1	Philippines	1·9
Colombia	8·0	South Korea	0·5
Egypt	0·5	Spain	8·3
Ghana	1·4	Taiwan	0·4
Greece	4·6	Thailand	1·2
India	1·2	Turkey	5·2
Israel	9·8	Venezuela	27·3
Malaya	1·6	Yugoslavia	3·1

Source: A. Maddison, *op. cit.*, p. 51.

cent. This had major repercussions of a depressive character else-where in the economy.

(*d*) The armed forces now number one million. This is five times their peacetime strength in British India. In 1968 India spent 3·7 per cent of national income for military purposes, compared with 1·5 per cent under the British raj in 1938. The military absorb scarce administrative talent, technical skills, the products of sophisticated domestic industry and a large volume of imports (whose cost is disguised by the artificially low official exchange rate). If India cut down military spending to what it was in the colonial period, it could use the resources saved to accelerate growth. On the other hand, Indian military expenditure is not much higher than the average for developing countries.

(e) There are institutional constraints on development which are more significant than in most other countries and act as 'built-in depressors'.[1] These include a ritual rather than functional attitude to work, the idea that manual labour is polluting, caste restrictions on job mobility, the backward position of women, scheduled castes and tribes, maldistribution of agricultural land, widespread incidence of sharecropping, and the taboo on cow slaughter which hinders efficient husbandry, linguistic divisions and regional jealousies.

None of the first four reasons are overwhelming disadvantages and some economists would not even acknowledge their validity. The importance of the fifth point is a matter of considerable controversy. It is difficult to distinguish between rigid institutional constraints and policy failures due to reluctance to attack institutions which would probably yield to pressure. Even if (e) is defined fairly broadly, it seems unlikely that these special constraints could account for the whole of the difference between Indian post-war growth and that of other countries. I have concluded elsewhere (with the help of a crude model) that India's autonomous (i.e. non-policy induced) growth potential was about 1·2 per cent below the average for a sample of twenty-two developing countries from 1950 to 1965.[2] As the average growth for these sample countries was about 5·5 per cent a year and Indian growth has been only 3·3 per cent a year we can conclude, after allowing for 1·2 per cent handicap, that better economic policy could have increased growth by 1 per cent a year, i.e. that India's growth potential was 4·3 per cent a year, and not the 3·3 per cent which was actually achieved.

[1] The phrase is Daniel Thorner's. See his *The Agrarian Prospect in India*, Delhi School of Economics, 1956. He considers that the combination of a hierarchical layer of land rights plus moneylender's claims have squeezed the actual 'tiller' so severely that he had no surplus to spare for investment nor any incentive to invest as his tenure was insecure. The possible interest of upper castes in increasing their income was offset by their reluctance to involve themselves with physical labour or with people who do it. Thorner does not think that these old attitudes had been changed by zamindari reform, though it seems obvious that the new technology has increased the incentive for landowners to exploit land as efficiently as possible.

[2] See A. Maddison, *Economic Progress and Policy in Developing Countries*, Allen and Unwin, London, 1970, for a detailed statistical analysis of the impact of policy on growth.

There have been several deficiencies in economic policy:

(*a*) Agrarian reform was not carried far enough; inequality of ownership, the poor legal status of sharecroppers, and the excessive number of landless labourers continued to act as built-in depressers.

(*b*) From 1955 onwards the government financed a major expansion of heavy industry. By 1968, investment in this sector by government amounted to Rs. 39 billion, i.e. over $5 billion, but the performance of these enterprises was poor. The product mix was wrong, and the state enterprises were badly run. This investment has produced small economic benefits in relation to the effort. In each of the years 1966 to 1969 these enterprises taken as a whole have made a loss.

(*c*) The government has given financial help to small industry and handicrafts, and prevented competition from firms in the modern sector. This has involved some waste of resources and poor quality goods, particularly textiles.

(*d*) The government has imposed detailed controls over resource allocation and prices in the private sector which have led to inefficiency (as acknowledged in the Fourth Plan).

(*e*) The exchange rate was greatly overvalued until 1966, and is still considerably overvalued. This made it necessary to impose tight physical controls on the allocation of imports and has severely checked the growth of exports. An attempt has been made to produce everything that it is physically possible to produce in India. Hence potential gains from international specialization have been lost.

These criticisms of policy are elaborated in the course of the next chapter, so no attempt is made to prove the points in more detail here. It should be stressed, however, that Indian growth policy has not fallen down because of a conflict between growth and equity. This is true of point (*c*) but not for any of the other points. Inequality is greater in India than in most Western capitalist countries and some of the policies which have hindered growth have also fostered inequality. This is true of controls over private sector industry (point (*d*)). In fact it can be argued that a more far-reaching land reform would have led to faster growth. Again this point is taken up in the next chapter.

Pakistan

Since independence, Pakistan's growth rate has probably accelerated more than that of India. From 1948 to 1969, national product has grown by 3·8 per cent a year.[1] In the colonial period it is possible

[1] See Table B-4 of Appendix B. In fact the figures on growth of aggregate

that the area which is now Pakistan had a somewhat higher growth rate than British India on a whole, but we cannot be sure of this. This is certainly true of West Pakistan, where agricultural output was growing much faster than elsewhere in India, but it could well be that this was offset by slower growth in East Bengal. In any case, the difference in post-war growth rates between East and West Pakistan has been very striking. From 1948 to 1969, East Pakistan grew by only 2·6 per cent a year, and West Pakistan by 4·5 per cent. Population has grown by 2·5 per cent a year in both areas. *Per capita* income has grown by 2 per cent a year in the West and not at all in the East. East Pakistan's aggregate growth has been higher since independence than before, but its *per capita* record has been the same as in the colonial period. It seems virtually certain that the average income level in East Pakistan is lower now than in 1757, for at that time Dacca was the capital of Bengal and the great centre of the luxury handicraft industry of Moghul India.

In India, the growth rate was higher in the 1950s than in the 1960s, but the reverse is true in Pakistan. In the 1950s the G.N.P. growth rate was only 2·6 per cent, whereas in the 1960s it was around 5·6 per cent. Slow growth in the 1950s had several causes. The Pakistan economy was much more strongly affected by partition than that of India. Refugees were 10 per cent of the population instead of 2 per cent as in India. In West Pakistan they were 20 per cent of the population. Production and property relations were badly disturbed and many of the people who left were those with essential skills. The economy was worse hit than India's by the cessation of trade between the two countries. Export markets for wheat, rice, jute and cotton disappeared, and this was the main reason for the stagnation of agriculture in the 1950s.

In the long run, some of these changes were beneficial. Immigrants are more enterprising and energetic than people who have always stayed at home. The exodus of Hindus in East Pakistan led to a quicker zamindari reform than in India, and the fact that the whole commercial and industrial structure had to be created from scratch created greater opportunities for enterprising people than in India. There were also fewer of the old hands in the civil service and a little less of the dead hand of tradition. Thus the disturbances of the 1950s were advantages of the 1960s, and some of the growth in the latter

---

output in India and Pakistan have only limited comparability. The figures for India refer to net domestic product (national income) whereas those for Pakistan refer to Gross National Product. Apart from this conceptual difference there are also differences in statistical procedure, e.g. in the treatment of small firms, which affect the comparability of the figures.

decade can probably be attributed to once-for-all elements of recovery.

Before comparing the efficiency of growth policy in Pakistan and in India, it is necessary to ask whether Pakistan's growth *potential* was likely to be different from that of India. We may review the factors which affected growth potential as follows:

(*a*) Pakistan's absolute income level is lower than that in India,[1] although the differential is not great. However, Pakistan had a very unusual economic structure at independence as it had virtually no industry or commerce. Hence, one might well argue that in the Pakistani case the 'advantages of backwardness' (which arise by catching up and copying the rest of the world), outweighed the disadvantages (i.e. those which are due to greater difficulties in resource mobilization).

(*b*) Pakistan's foreign aid has been bigger proportionately than that of India. Virtually all the benefits of foreign aid have gone to West Pakistan, which has done quite well by international standards.

(*c*) Pakistan's overall natural resource endowment is probably worse than that of India, but agriculture is not subject to such great instability. Half of West Pakistan's agricultural land was irrigated at the time of independence (three-quarters now), and East Pakistan's problem is one of floods rather than droughts, but the floods are not usually as catastrophic as Indian droughts.

(*d*) Pakistani military expenditures are somewhat bigger than those of India.

(*e*) Pakistan has fewer traditional obstacles to growth than India. Caste restrictions are weaker and are not sanctioned by religion, the old society got more of a shakeup during the partition period, and taboos on efficient animal husbandry are rather unimportant. However, the position of women is more backward in Pakistan than in India, and their participation in the labour force is minimal.

On the whole, therefore, it would seem that Pakistan's growth potential might be somewhat higher than that of India, though few people would have argued this way twenty years ago, and one could hardly claim that Pakistan's advantage was very substantial.

Like India, Pakistan has grown more slowly than the average for developing countries, and the gap is too big to be explained entirely by constraints exogenous to economic policy. We must therefore conclude that Pakistani policy was deficient, though less so than that of India. The main deficiencies have been as follows:

[1] West Pakistan's *per capita* income is higher, East Pakistan's lower than that of India.

(*a*) Lack of any clear economic policy for development in the period up to 1958, imposition of price controls which were a severe deterrent to agriculture, maintenance of a detailed mechanism of industrial control which harmed allocation of domestic resources;

(*b*) maintenance of a highly overvalued exchange rate and a trade boycott with India. The degree of overvaluation has been greater than in India since 1966, but is mitigated by the bonus voucher scheme for exports which produces the same effect as a multiple floating exchange rate for some transactions.

The ideological flavour of Pakistani governments has been quite different from that in India. For this reason, whenever there has been a conflict between economic growth and equity, the latter has usually been sacrificed without hesitation. By contrast with India's 'socialist pattern', the official Pakistani doctrine has been one of functional inequality, i.e. inequality has been regarded as a positive virtue. Thus income tax has been kept low, business has had a free hand to develop monopolistic groups, public enterprises were created for functional rather than ideological reasons, there has been no nationalization, no programmes for village uplift, and trade union leaders have been imprisoned. East Pakistan has been neglected to concentrate resources in the West. When there was land reform in West Pakistan, the ceiling on holdings was fixed at 500 acres instead of 50 acres as is generally the upper limit in India. In East Pakistan, land reform derived from the political accident that zamindars were Hindus rather than from any social pressures. The only 'social' programme of any size was the Works Programme in East Pakistan, and this was adopted largely under foreign pressure.

Chapter VI

The Social Impact of India's 'Socialist Pattern'

India emerged at independence with a political party strong enough to hold power continuously for a quarter of a century and has had socialist Prime Ministers (father and daughter), for almost the whole period. The proclaimed aim of policy since independence has been to create a 'socialist pattern of society' by non-revolutionary methods. Most elements of the policy were a reflection of Nehru's views, but it also incorporated concessions to Gandhi's utopian doctrines about village society and the virtues of primitive technology. The main components of this 'socialist' policy were as follows:

(a) abolition of the privileges of princes (with compensation);
(b) abolition of zamindari tenures (with compensation) and land reform;
(c) a sharp increase in the (theoretic) progressivity of income tax;
(d) measures to improve the social status of backward classes (untouchables and tribal people) and women;
(e) programmes of village uplift—community development, co-operatives, etc.;
(f) measures to promote small-scale industry and revive hand-loom textiles;
(g) creation of a public sector and imposition of detailed controls on the private sector in industry;
(h) rapid development of heavy industry;
(i) rapid expansion of education facilities.

Serious action was taken to implement all these policies, but the results can hardly be described as socialism. Some of the Gandhian programmes have been predictable failures, particularly those based on revival of the village 'community' or of obsolete technologies. Civic rights legislation to rehabilitate untouchables or upgrade the status of women is necessarily slow in making a significant impact. The removal of princes and zamindars was an undeniable success, but their privileges were so anachronistic that they do not appear (in retrospect) as very formidable targets. Basically the 'socialist pattern' has disappointed, because it has done little to help those at the bottom of society, i.e. landless labourers and poor peasants who are about half of the population. There is no evidence that the range of income inequality has narrowed. The effective tax burden of the upper income groups has remained low. Controls over the private sector have promoted the interest of large monopoly groups. The colonial structure of the army and the bureaucracy have been left untouched. The economy is less 'feudal' and more capitalist, but it is a bureaucratically controlled and inefficient capitalism. The so-called 'socialist pattern' has done nothing to speed up economic growth. There is no doubt that growth has been better than in the colonial period, but it might well have been faster still without the 'socialist pattern'.

Figures on income distribution are rather poor. In 1960 the Planning Commission set up a committee (the Mahalanobis Committee) to inquire into the problem which took nine years to complete its report.[1] The estimates of income distribution cited by the committee are shown in Table VI-1. They show a degree of income inequality before tax higher than exists in capitalist countries like the U.K. or U.S.A.[2] Furthermore, the tax system of most Western countries does more to redistribute income. In 1965 the U.K. collected 16·1 per cent of national product in direct taxes, most of which are highly progressive; the U.S.A. collected 18 per cent.[3] In India, direct taxes were only 2·8 per cent of national income in 1967, so very little redistribution is attained by this means. In agriculture there is no income tax at all in most states and land tax is not progressive. In urban areas there is a progressive income tax which rises to quite high rates, but less than 1 per cent of the population pay it, there is widespread evasion, and the higher bureaucracy and military have large tax-free perquisites. The Mahalanobis report acknowledged that income tax has a negligible impact on income distribution. The top 20 per cent in urban areas keep 56·2 per cent of income after tax, compared with 57·6 per cent before tax. The Indian Government makes very few income transfers to households except civil service and military pensions, privy purses to princes and compensation payments to zamindars. The main government expenditures for social purposes are those on health and education. These items amounted to 3·2 per cent of national income in 1968. But if one looks closely at health and education, the main beneficiaries

---

[1] See Planning Commission, *Report of the Committee on Distribution of Income and Levels of Living*, Part I, Delhi, 1964; Part II, Delhi, 1969.

[2] See S. Kuznets, 'Distribution of Income by Size', *Economic Development and Cultural Change*, January 1963.

[3] See A. Maddison, *Economic Progress and Policy in Developing Countries*, Allen and Unwin, London, 1970, p. 73.

are the upper income groups in urban areas, who are the main users of expensive universities and hospitals. In terms of income distribution and fiscal policy, it is therefore difficult to discern any 'socialist' element in the Indian situation.

Table VI-1

Percentage Distribution of Pre-tax Household
Income in India in 1960

Percentage of households	Percentage of income	
	Urban	Rural
0–10	1·3	0·7
10–20	2·7	3·3
20–30	3·6	4·5
30–40	4·5	5·6
40–50	5·4	6·6
50–60	6·5	7·7
60–70	8·1	9·5
70–80	10·3	12·1
80–90	15·2	16·4
90–100	42·4	33·6

Sources: Planning Commission, *Report of the Committee on Distribution of Income and Levels of Living*, Part I, Delhi, February 1964, p. 27.

The Mahalanobis report did not find enough evidence to decide whether the degree of income inequality had increased or decreased in the 1950s, and it did not even present any data for the 1960s. It did give some figures on the growth of individual items of consumption which were designed to support the hypothesis that the fruits of economic growth have filtered down to the mass of the population. But the interpretation of the basic data led some of the committee to dissent, and one of the claims of the Mahalanobis report which passed unchallenged, i.e. that *per capita* clothing consumption increased by 64 per cent from 1950 to 1960, seems to be quite incorrect.[1] A more recent report, commissioned by the Ford

[1] See Planning Commission, *Report of the Committee on Distribution of Income and Levels of Living*, Part II, *Changes in Levels of Living*, Delhi, 1969, page 7 refers to cotton clothing, page 56 refers to cotton cloth. The Ministry of Finance, *Economic Survey 1969–70*, Delhi, 1970, p. 74 shows a 28 per cent increase in *per capita* consumption of cloth from 1951 to 1968. *Per capita* production of yarn increased by only 15 per cent from 1950 to 1968 so even the Ministry of Finance figure is probably an overstatement if allowance is made for the fall in quality as a result of the increased role of khadi and hand-loom weaving.

Foundation,[1] concludes that inequality increased in the 1960s, with a marked deterioration in the standards of the urban poor.

Because the reality of India's 'socialism' is so different from the rhetoric, many observers have accused Nehru of hypocrisy. Gunnar Myrdal has characterized India as a 'soft state' unable to implement socialist goals: 'the combination of radicalism in principle and conservatism in practice, the signs of which were already apparent in the Congress before independence, was quickly woven into the fabric of Indian politics. Social legislation pointed the direction in which society should travel, but left the pace indeterminate. Many of these laws were intentionally permissive.'[2] However, the hypocrisy charge against Nehru is unfair, because it credits him with more power than he had. India has been governed since independence by a coalition consisting of the bureaucratic-military establishment, which implements policy, the big business groups which have backed Congress financially, the rank-and-file politicians who mainly represent the rural squirearchy and richer peasants, and the intellectuals who articulate policy. Nehru belonged to the fourth group, which was the weakest but most vocal. His position as Prime Minister was very much the same as the one he occupied in the pre-war Congress party. He was a leftist flanked by conservatives who knew from experience that it was not worth opposing progressive resolutions or legislation which were not likely to be implemented.

The important charge against Nehru is not hypocrisy but strategic error. He obviously could not have achieved all his social aims without breaking up the system of parliamentary democracy, but he expended a good deal of the political leverage he did have and used too much of the country's resources to build up a bureaucratically controlled industrial sector and a wide range of inefficient heavy industries in the name of socialism. For him this industrial strategy was a surrogate for social change, although it did nothing to promote equality or economic growth. It won support from the bureaucratic establishment because it added to their power, it was supported by politicians because it increased their patronage, it met no opposition from established industry because it did not interfere with vested interests and it was supported by intellectuals who generally identified

[1] See V. M. Dandekar and N. Rath, *Poverty in India*, Economic and Political Weekly, Bombay, 1971.

[2] See G. Myrdal, *Asian Drama*, Pantheon, 1968, p. 276. Myrdal is not the only one to deplore the gap between the alleged objectives of Indian policy and its practical achievements. Many Indians feel the same way, including Professor D. R. Gadgil, who is now Deputy Chairman of the Planning Commission. See D. R. Gadgil, *Planning and Economic Policy in India*, Asia Publishing House, Bombay, 1962.

capitalism with colonialism, and who assumed that government control would contribute to social justice. It aroused no opposition because it conflicted with no vested interests. But there were other politically feasible options which could have done more for both social justice and economic growth, i.e. a less dirigiste industrial policy and a more vigorous attempt to push land redistribution either through land reform or fiscal policy.

The main social changes which have occurred since independence have been at the top. There has been a complete displacement of the British from the bureaucratic military establishment, and a big reduction in the importance of British capitalists and managerial personnel in the private sector. Thus the foreign claim of about 5 per cent of national income which existed in the colonial period has been drastically reduced, and the corresponding share of national income has been taken over by the indigenous elite of civil servants, military, capitalists and professional people. The old Moghul remnants, the princes and zamindars, have been stripped of social status but financially compensated. There was an element of confiscation in their treatment, but less than one might have expected; financially they are still in the top 1 per cent of the population. These Moghul remnants are gradually assimilating into the new elite of capitalists and professionals, and this process will be speeded up with the final disappearance of the social privileges of princes in 1970. It might well be the case that the top 1 per cent of the population get a little less of the cake than they did in colonial times, and that some of the income benefits of decolonization have filtered down to the rest of the population and particularly to the village squirearchy and the small pampered group of workers in public enterprise. However, little has been done since independence which is likely to have made any significant difference to the real income of the bottom three layers of the rural population, i.e. the tribal population, the landless labourers, and the poorest layers of peasants who own less than 2·5 acres of land. These people form more than half of the population and have benefited only from token programmes, and what Doreen Warriner calls 'feeble do-goodism'. Until a real land reform gives them some stake in the economy, most of them will get virtually no benefit from economic growth. All they have to sell is their labour and the price of this is not rising in a labour surplus economy.

Although these facts about Indian development are officially admitted, plan documents sometimes suggest that economic growth (what little there has been) produces a gradual 'filtering-down' effect on mass consumption. Thus the Third Plan says (p. 17): 'with rapid development and expansion of employment, the incomes of the vast majority of workers in industry and services and of self-employed workers like farmers and skilled artisans may be expected to rise steadily, and on the whole, in fair relationship to productivity'. The document does have some reservations about the fate of those with fixed incomes, or the unemployed, but does not mention landless labourers. This filtering-down theory of economic growth is about as unrealistic in Indian conditions as Macaulay's 140-year-old optimism that knowledge of the English language would filter down.

In the Fourth Plan document there is a change of tone. The filtering-down theory is not mentioned. It is now argued that equality is the enemy of growth in the short term. The Fourth Plan states (p. 15): 'In a rich country greater equality could be achieved in part through transfer of income through fiscal, pricing and other policies. No significant results can be achieved through such measures in a poor country, where whatever surpluses can be mobilized from the higher incomes of the richer classes are needed for investment in the economy to lay the basis for larger consumption in the future.' This 'pie-in-the-sky' approach to growth strategy comes rather close to the Pakistani ideology of 'functional inequality', which is examined in the next chapter. It is not a very convincing doctrine in a country where the rich save so little[1] and where half the population is so poor that their working capacity is substantially affected by how much they eat.

1. *Politicians*
The immediate beneficiaries of Indian independence were the professional politicians who took over the power previously enjoyed by the British raj and the Indian princes.

At independence, about 47 per cent of the area of the country consisted of autonomous principalities, which are now integral parts of the Indian union. Hyderabad put up armed resistance, and there was conflict with Pakistan over Kashmir. Elsewhere the transfer was achieved peacefully with the help of generous privy purses, diplomatic privileges in respect of income tax, customs duty, retention of honorary titles, salutes, etc., which were abolished only in 1970. Apart from their privy purses, many of the princes have large private fortunes, and some of them still live like Moghul princes. However, their share of national income has probably fallen and most of them are becoming modern capitalists, managers, professional men and politicians.

The second major change was the reorganization of state boun-

[1] In 1967, domestic savings were only 8 per cent of national income, about half the U.S. level and a quarter of that in Japan.

daries on a linguistic basis. There are now seventeen states (as well as ten centrally-administered union territories). Their creation has strengthened regional loyalties and weakened the Centre. For this reason the reorganization was resisted by Nehru until 1956. India now has a looser federal system than the U.S.A., U.S.S.R. or Brazil. This has had important policy consequences and has left the Central Government fairly impotent in important social fields such as land reform and agricultural taxation.

Another change since independence has been the introduction of universal suffrage. The 1952 electorate was more than five times as large as in 1935. Usually one-half of the electorate vote. In the long run this means that the backward classes should make their voice felt, but until recently they have been rather inarticulate and are, of course, a minority.

Since independence, stress has been placed on the role of elected village councils (panchayats). These are generally ineffective because they have little financial power and are dominated by the traditionally dominant groups in the village. Since 1959, groups of village panchayats choose representatives for a council at block level (*panchayat samiti*) and at district level (*zila parishad*), and these committees are a useful check on bureaucratic power in some areas, particularly Maharashtra and Gujarat.

The political network includes about 800 members of parliament for the two houses (Lok Sabha and Rajya Sabha) at the centre, and 3,200 members of the legislative assemblies (most states have two houses) in the states. In addition, there are politicians in local government, and political activists in the party machine. About 1,000 politicians hold ministerial office.

The dominant party has been the Congress which represented a very wide range of interest groups, but there are many other parties ranging from the Right-wing Swatantra party (created in 1959), the Jan Sangh (Hindu nationalist party founded in 1951) to the two communist parties which participate in electoral politics.[1] Apart from the national parties, there are some strong regional parties such as the DMK in Madras and the Akali Dal in Punjab. The Congress party has now split into two major factions. The majority faction led by Mrs Gandhi is aligned with the Left and has carried out some new populist measures such as bank nationalization and termination of

[1] In the first general election in 1952, Congress won 362 of the 489 seats in the Lok Sabha. In the fourth general election in 1967, Congress got 275 out of 520 seats, Swatantra 44, Jan Sangh 35, DMK 25, Lohia socialists 23, Right communists 22 and Left communists 19. See H. Tinker, *India and Pakistan*, Pall Mall, London, 1967, pp. 49 and 66.

the privy purses for princes, whilst the minority faction of the old Congress is primarily a Right-wing group.

Politicians come from all social classes and are less Westernized and less intellectual than those who led the struggle for independence. The dominant social group which has emerged is the village squire-archy and rich peasants, the intermediate group of non-brahmin non-untouchables whose main goal is their own material interest. Regionalism has also made politics more parochial and more influenced by caste considerations. In South India, particularly in Madras and Mysore, they threw out the previously dominant group of brahmins who were allied with Congress. They have less interest in furthering the interests of the untouchables than did the old Westernized leadership of Congress. It is the power of this group which helped to block effective land reform or any realistic level of agricultural income tax. Indian political activity is now largely centred on the struggle to attain office, and there is little organized extra-parliamentary voluntary activity to improve civil rights or achieve social reform as there was in the days of Gandhi.

Politicians get official salaries and may also get official housing, but the material rewards are not very substantial. Most politicians affect simple khadi dress. Ministers get lavish housing, servants and official cars. At the centre, some of the old British-Moghul pomp still exists with the President living in the Viceroy's house. However, Nehru's palatial old Prime Ministerial residence is now a museum and ministerial pomp is declining.

2. *The Bureaucracy*

The bureaucracy is a legacy from the British raj. It is an autocratic power structure devised by the British as the 'steel frame' of their Imperial power.

Because of the existence of a vigorous group of politicians, free elections, a free press, and a fairly loose federal system, the bureau-cracy is not as powerful in framing policy at the 'secretariat' level as it was in the British raj, but the 'socialist pattern' has greatly widened its economic responsibility. At the district level, the changes have so far been small and, if anything, have strengthened the power of the civil service. Since independence, government employees have risen in number from 3 million to 9·9 million in December 1968.[1]

Nehru had written before independence, 'of one thing I am quite

[1] In 1968 there were 2·7 million at the Centre, 3·8 million in the states, 1·8 million in local government, and 1·5 million in paragovernmental agencies. See Ministry of Finance, *Pocket Book of Economic Information 1969*, Delhi, 1970. For the figure at independence, see S. Sivasubramonian, *op. cit.*

sure, that no new order can be built up in India so long as the spirit of the I.C.S. pervades our administration and our public services. . . . Therefore it seems to me quite essential that the I.C.S. and similar services must disappear completely, as such, before we can start real work on a new order. Individual members of these services, if they are willing and competent for the new jobs, will be welcome, but only on new conditions.'[1]

There were three main reasons why the bureaucratic pattern was not changed at independence. Firstly, the British had insisted as a condition of independence that India guarantee the traditional privileges of higher civil servants. Secondly, the risks of dismantling the structure were great when the country had just been partitioned and the princely states had yet to be absorbed. Thirdly, the civil service was already largely Indianized and the bureaucrats were generally sympathetic to the aims of the Congress governments. There is no doubt, however, that the bureaucratic structure is now an anachronism which conflicts with some of the major aims of social policy.

In the first place, a government which is committed to creating a casteless, classless society should have a bureaucratic system which sets the right tone. Instead, civil servants are segregated into four classes which maintain an almost ritual distance from each other. Power is highly concentrated on the 17,231 officers in Class I of the Central Government who are less than 1 per cent of the total strength of 2·7 million. Within Class I, the 2,500 members of the I.A.S. (Indian Administrative Service) stand out as the super-elite. At independence there were 1,157 officers in the I.C.S., of which only about half were Indians, so the number of Indians in the super-elite has increased about fivefold. The I.A.S. are mainly recruited by examination at the age of twenty-one or twenty-two, although there have been some lateral entrants. Most upper Indian civil servants were brahmins until independence. Now their caste origins are more diverse and there are a few ex-untouchables amongst them, but their training, status, perquisites and power preserve the old elitist attitudes.

Class II officers have the same basic educational qualifications as Class I, and most of them are people who failed the Class I examinations. As a result they face a lifetime of subordinate status, pay and responsibility.

Most of the Class III staff are clerical workers whose working language is English. Usually they have only a half knowledge of this language, so that their work is done mechanically, with only quasi-

[1] See J. Nehru, *An Autobiography*, Allied Publishers, Bombay, 1962, p. 445.

comprehension of its functional purpose. In most countries the majority of Class III personnel would be women but, in India, women's liberation has only affected the upper class.

Class IV consists of more than a million menials—functionally redundant guards and bearers (*chaprasis*) who carry tea and files and salute their officers. Most of their time is spent loitering in corridors. One calculation suggests that on average they are usefully employed for twelve minutes a day. The rest of their time is spent reducing the productivity of Class III. Some government departments find it easier to function when most of them are absent on casual leave, otherwise the offices would be too crowded and there would not be enough chairs.

The basic unit of administration is the district and power is still heavily concentrated on the district officer, who is the chief tax collector and policeman and allocator of development funds. The district officer still has a paternalist role at the local level and his status is similar to what it was under the British raj. District officers belong to the all-India service and are not too dependent on local politicians for promotion. Rather the local politicians are dependent on civil servants for favours. This is particularly so because local government has practically no funds of its own but must rely on state and central funds. There are 560,000 villages in India and only 320 districts, so the average district officer or sub-divisional officer will have a wide choice as to which village will get favours such as a road, a tubewell, a school or a health centre. In the long run, the growth in elected local government should moderate the power of district commissioners and their agents—the police, tax collectors and village level workers—who may become servants rather than masters of these local government bodies. This is not the case yet at village level but there has been some change at the district level where there are effective zila parishads which have taken over development functions as in Mahrashtra.[1] In municipal government, the effective power of officials nominated by state governments is still large, and municipal areas are also within the control of district officers.

As a result of this dominance of local administration by the old bureaucratic elite, the pattern of expenditure on social services tends to favour the interests of the upper income groups. Wherever there is no clear political directive the bias of the system in allocating favours is always inegalitarian and conservative.

At the secretariat level, the civil service is now subject to ministerial directive, parliamentary question, press comment, and official com-

[1] See Administrative Reforms Commission, *District Administration*, Delhi, February 1967.

missions of enquiry, so its position is not as strong as in Pakistan or under the British raj. However, the British operated a system of minimal government in a *laissez-faire* economy chiefly concerned with law and order, whereas the state now has much larger economic responsibilities, with detailed controls over the private sector, and responsibility for a large number of public enterprises. All these new responsibilities have had to be handled by a civil service whose basic structure has remained the same. Because of the low level of competence of most of the civil service below Class I, economic efficiency is greatly hindered by the Dickensian bumbledum of chit-signing, file-pushing and absurdly detailed and repetitive ledger-keeping. No big decision can be taken without mountains of paper and many small decisions require a bribe. The main sufferers are consumers and some would-be entrepreneurs. Large-scale business can afford to pay the go-betweens who are necessary to make the system work.

Since independence there has been a steady and substantial erosion of the real value of salaries of higher civil servants, and income tax is a fairly heavy burden, which was not the case in pre-independence years. This makes civil servants very keen on perquisites such as subsidized official housing, and as perquisites are tax free they are now a very important part of real income as well as significant and overt badges of status.

'Government officials in India are given residential accommodation, a practice which evidently grew out of the need to provide reasonably comfortable living conditions for British civil servants living in an alien country. In New Delhi today, a commodious house in an exclusive neighbourhood is one of the chief perquisites of a government official. Houses, and the areas in which they are located, are graded in an elaborate hierarchy. Secretaries live in spacious bungalows with front and back lawns, and for others there are houses ranging from Type A to Type G. Type A houses, mainly for Additional and Joint Secretaries, have six rooms, garages and servants' quarters; at the other end, there is provision of two- and one-roomed accommodation for lower division clerks and menial staff.

'Not only are the houses different in character, but they are generally located in different areas, whose very names often signify gradations of status.'[1]

[1] See A. Beteille, *Castes: Old and New*, Asia Publishing House, Bombay, 1969, pp. 234–5. The same point is made by M. N. Srinivas, *op. cit.*, p. 94: 'Foreign social scientists are astonished that residential quarters built by the Government of India for its employees in Delhi should observe the hierarchical principle so scrupulously.'

The senior bureaucracy (and military) not only get substantial perquisites in housing, but generally live in areas in which urban amenities are subsidized and are much superior than for the population generally. These amenities are usually subsidized by the rest of the population. The pattern dates from colonial times, but there has been no real move to change it. The situation now is still the same as that described by Nehru when he was Chairman of the Allahabad Municipality, except that Indians have replaced the English officials and businessmen.

'Most Indian cities can be divided into two parts: the densely crowded city proper, and the widespread area with bungalows and cottages, each with a fairly extensive compound or garden, usually referred to by the English as the "Civil Lines". It is in these Civil Lines that the English officials and businessmen, as well as many upper middle-class Indians, professional men, officials, etc., live. The income of the municipality from the city proper is greater than from the Civil Lines, but the expenditure on the latter far exceeds the city expenditure. For the far wider area covered by the Civil Lines requires more roads, and they have to be repaired, cleaned-up, watered, and lighted; and the drainage, the water supply, and the sanitation system have to be more widespread. The city part is always grossly neglected, and, of course, the poorer parts of the city are almost ignored; it has few good roads, and most of the narrow lanes are ill-lit and have no proper drainage or sanitation system.'[1]

In order to mitigate the inequality a little, Nehru wanted to introduce a tax on land values, but was prevented by the district magistrate. Instead of taxing the rich by this mechanism, municipalities relied on *octroi* (a tax on goods in transit) which falls most heavily on the poor. The situation in this respect has not changed much since independence.

The trouble about these perquisites is that they isolate the higher bureaucracy from the problems of ordinary people, and reduce their sense of urgency about social problems. A Class I officer will usually live in a cantonment area with superior public amenities. He will travel by private car and is unlikely to use any public transport except the state airline. He will stay in a government hostel, rest house, or circuit house when on tour, seldom in a hotel. When he is ill he goes to a hospital for civil servants. He works in a language which most people do not understand. His children usually go to private schools. To some extent this is an inevitable result of the

[1] See J. Nehru, *An Autobiography*, Allied Publishers, Bombay, 1962, p. 143.

extreme poverty of the country, and without the perquisites efficiency would drop sharply in many situations. But these privileges reduce bureaucratic incentives to build up the social infrastructure. Everyone with power or responsibility in the establishment is protected from harsh realities which are the daily lot of the mass of the population. The segregation is almost as great as in colonial times. If those at the top had to use normal school, hospital or public transport facilities, they would be more eager to improve them. There is, therefore, a strong case for reducing perquisites and, if necessary, compensating for their loss by pay increases.

Apart from 'legitimate' perquisites, there is a fair amount of official corruption. On lower levels this was always widespread even in colonial times, but the opportunities now are much greater because of the enlarged role of government in the economy. Amongst Class I civil servants, corruption seems to be rare, but there has not yet been the same political incentive to pry into its incidence as closely as was the case in Pakistan in 1958 and 1969.

The structure, functions and personnel of the civil service have been under lengthy review from the Administrative Reforms Commission since 1966, and a number of proposals for change have emerged from its numerous reports, study groups and working parties. The main proposals are:

(a) to end the present multiplicity of grades and rigid segregation into four classes and create a simplified and uniform system of twenty–twenty-five grades;

(b) to increase the amount spent on in-service training (from 0·4 to 1·0 per cent of the salary bill);

(c) to establish promotion quotas and facilitate movement between grades;

(d) to introduce procedures which will make it possible to fire people who are inefficient or redundant (with compensation);

(e) to keep the present concentration of 'civil' functions on the district officer but to spread his economic responsibilities amongst elected bodies and functional specialists;

(f) to establish more efficient auditing procedures;

(g) to create a separate cadre of management for nationalized industry with a separate pay scale rising to Rs. 4,000 a month instead of Rs. 2,500 as at present.

Most of these are useful suggestions and they would help promote efficiency and social justice if they were implemented. However, the Commission stops short at some fundamental problems. It does not attack the present system of perquisites in the form of housing.

Rather it suggests that these privileges be extended. It is also against any major increase in pay for top level officers and suggests 3,500 rupees a month as a maximum. There is no proposal for improving professional performance by enlarging the top echelons and retrenchment of menial personnel. Although it is acknowledged that the management of nationalized industries needs improvement,[1] the present system of bureaucratic control over the private sector receives general endorsement.[2]

The main failing of the civil service is not that it is too big or too well paid, but that it is an autocratic Anglo-Brahmin structure created to run a static economy. At the top level, rewards come in the form of perquisites and mandarin social status, and increasingly in the form of bribes. There is an obvious need for higher pay, fewer perquisites and a bigger cadre. The rigid caste-like segregation between classes and services should be replaced by a simplified system of grades with greater provision for job mobility and in-service training. There is unlikely to be much social mobility in the private sector as long as immobility is institutionalized in the public sector. The civil service should also make a bigger effort to hire women as an example to the private sector. Most of the flunkeys and guards in Class IV should be pensioned off.

3. *The Military*
Like the bureaucracy, the armed forces are a heritage of the British raj. At the time of partition there were about 230,000 in the armed forces allotted to India.[3] The number rose to 550,000 in 1962, but was strengthened after the conflict with China, and since then has risen to more than one million. The number of Indian officers has risen more than sixfold since independence—because in 1947 half of the officers were still British who have been replaced. There are now 40,000 officers compared with 406 Indians in 1938. The armed forces have changed less than the civil service since independence and are still very similar to what the British left. Their political status has been reduced by abolishing the office of commander-in-chief and subordinating the forces to civilian ministers. Training for the armed forces is now free, so recruitment of officers is open to a wider range of society, but promotion from the ranks is rare. Promotion to

[1] See Administrative Reforms Commission, *Public Sector Undertakings*, Delhi, October 1967.

[2] See Administrative Reforms Commission, *Economic Administration*, July 1968.

[3] See A. L. Venkateswaran, *Defence Organization in India*, Ministry of Information and Broadcasting, Delhi, 1967.

'junior commissioned officer' is possible only from the ranks, but junior commissioned officers (*risaldars*, *subedar* majors and *subedars*) are really senior N.C.O.s who have no counterpart in the armed forces of any other country except Pakistan. The survival of this system may mitigate social inequality in the armed forces to some extent, but the existence of a double-thick hurdle of N.C.O.s makes it more difficult for a bright young recruit of lower-class origins to jump from the ranks to the officer corps.

There has been a deliberate attempt to break with the old tradition of martial races. There are now rather few Muslims in the armed forces but there are still a disproportionate number of sikhs, dogras, gurkhas, rajputs and other 'martial races'. There is a territorial army and a cadet corps in universities and colleges, but these are on the British pattern. There has been no attempt to use the army for development purposes or to introduce conscription. This is a pity, as the armed forces are extremely efficient and one of the most Westernized elements in Indian society. To some extent the Westernization is still Kiplingesque, but the important thing is that the armed forces are indifferent to caste.[1]

4. *Other Professions*

Since independence there has been a considerable expansion in the service sector of the economy and in the number of professional personnel. The number of engineers (graduates and diploma holders) has risen from 65,000 in 1951 to 330,000 in 1968, doctors from 62,000 to 103,000.[2] There are almost 100,000 teachers in higher education, about 62,000 scientists in research and development, about 3,000 journalists and about 50,000 lawyers. In total there are probably about a million people in these professional groups.[3] In general, these people have a high social status and considerable political influence. The intellectual community benefits from a long cultural tradition

[1] See A. Beteille, *Castes: Old and New*, p. 215, 'There is much there (the Air Force mess in Delhi) to remind one of the glories of the British Raj; the silver, the cut glass and the linen the same. Officers spend their evenings playing billiards or poker, and drinking beer, whisky or rum. Informal groups are formed with an almost complete indifference to the principles of caste.'

[2] See *Report of the Committee on Distribution of Income and Levels of Living*, Part II, p. 64, and Planning Commission, *Fourth Five Year Plan 1969–74*, Delhi, 1970.

[3] This is a rough guess. There is some information about these professional groups in E. Shils, *The Intellectual Between Tradition and Modernity*, Mouton, The Hague, 1961. There is also some information in B. B. Misra, *op. cit.*, but the numbers on the stock of such people in colonial and post-colonial times are surprisingly vague. The trouble is that the census includes workers like barbers, washermen and scavengers in this group.

and from the large size of the country. As a result there are intellectual centres such as Delhi or Aligarh universities and high quality news-papers which bear comparison with the best anywhere in the world.

5. *Agriculture*

Since independence there have been some important institutional changes in agriculture. The main change has been the removal of the last layer of fiscal 'intermediaries' left over from the Moghuls, i.e. the zamindars of Bengal, Bihar, Orissa and parts of Madras, the taluqdars of U.P., the jagirdars of the princely states, and the holders of *inams* (tax-free land). These people still held senior title to about 40 per cent of the land area at independence. Most of them were absentee landlords paying land revenue to the state governments and collecting rents from tenants. Under the legislation which the Central Government urged on the various state governments their land rights were taken over by the states from 1952 onwards, and they were given compensation which varied degressively with the size of their holding. There have been delays in payment, the interest payable on the compensation bonds is only $2\frac{1}{2}$ to 3 per cent, and compensation is not geared to the rising level of land prices and rents. There has, therefore, been a considerable element of confiscation in the arrange-ment though the capital component of compensation should ultimately be Rs. 5·1 billion.[1] The previous tenants of zamindars now pay land tax directly to the state governments and the rate of tax has been augmented to include the amount previously paid as rents to zamindars.

The main beneficiaries of these changes have been the old 'occupancy' tenants or 'tenants-in-chief' of zamindars. Most of these are higher caste peasants, and many of them are not working farmers, though they are called 'cultivators' in official documents. Under the British regime, most of these 'occupancy' tenants had secure tenure and rents which were low by the standards they themselves imposed on sub-tenants. Under the new regime they have even firmer titles, and their rent (the new land tax) burden has fallen in real terms as prices have risen. Land revenue is now less than 0·8 per cent of total agricultural income.[2]

Many of the ex-zamindars were not large landlords and were allowed to retain their land. Big zamindars were also allowed to retain some land which they had used previously as 'home farms'. In most cases they had not personally cultivated such land but had

[1] See Planning Commission, *Progress of Land Reform*, Delhi, 1963, p. 4.
[2] In 1969–70, land revenue was Rs. 1,176 million and farm income was about Rs. 150,000 million.

leased it to tenants-at-will. Most of these tenants were dispossessed and converted into sharecroppers, or landless labourers, because zamindars wanted to make their rights to such land as waterproof as possible. Furthermore, they could increase the area of such claims by allotting part of their lands to family members for 'cultivation'. The dispossession of tenants on 'home farms' could easily be pushed beyond its legal bounds because areas under 'Permanent Settlement' (of which there were more than 100 million acres) had no local revenue officials and no accurate records of tenant rights. Zamindars who did not have 'home farms' were usually able to acquire them before the legislation was implemented. It is not possible to make any accurate assessment of the proportion of land retained by zamindars in this way, but we may quote the experience in Bihar as an example. There, the area held by 'intermediaries' was 38·7 million acres (about 90 per cent of the area of the state). About 15 million acres appears to have been waste land which is now held by the state, and the other 23·7 million acres were cultivable land, of which zamindars retained about 7 per cent for their personal cultivation.[1] This 7 per cent was usually the best land. Unfortunately, there is no means of telling how typical Bihar's experience may have been, but I suspect that, in general, zamindari retentions were well above 7 per cent, because there were so many small zamindars in Bengal and U.P.

Under the new system there is still a complex hierarchy of ownership rights. The top layer of people holding land directly from the states, i.e. the ex-zamindars on their home farms, and their more privileged ex-tenants have virtually the same property rights as freehold landlords in a Western capitalist country. However, some of the ex-tenants of zamindars, who now hold their land rights directly from the state, have somewhat inferior titles. In U.P., which is the biggest state in India, 16·1 million acres are held by '*bhumidhars* (who have permanent, heritable and transferable rights)' and about 29·5 million acres by '*sirdars* (who have permanent and heritable rights but not the right of transfer)'. Thus even now the system is not quite capitalist, though sirdars can purchase the right to become bhumidhars at a somewhat exorbitant price.

Zamindari abolition in itself did nothing to help tenants-at-will, sharecroppers or landless labourers except in so far as the states have gained control of low-quality waste land which they can sell or distribute.[2] In fact, zamindari abolition dispossessed those tenants-at-will who held land resumed by zamindars as home farms. Further-

[1] See Planning Commission, National Development Council, *Implementation of Land Reforms*, New Delhi, August 1966.

[2] In the old ryotwari areas, the states already held rights over waste land.

more, these changes did not affect areas of ryotwari tenure (60 per cent of India).

In order to remedy this situation, the states (in both ryotwari and zamindari areas) were urged by the centre to take measures to give tenants greater security of tenure, and limit rents to a quarter of the crop (instead of half the crop which is the usual rate). All states did introduce such legislation, but the provisions vary a good deal, there are still several categories of tenant, and evasion is widespread. Forcible resumption of land for personal 'cultivation' is legally permitted up to certain limits, and a good deal of land has been resumed illegally or under the guise of voluntary surrenders. Before legislation was finalized, landlords had time to change their tenants or move them on to plots where they had no vested occupancy rights. Land records are usually poor, tenants have less access to government and are less able to afford litigation than are landlords. In some states, such as Kashmir, Madras, Punjab and West Bengal, the legal definition of a fair rent is up to half of gross produce. In most states rents are still payable in kind rather than cash. In U.P., where tenancy has been made illegal, landlords now lease out land entirely on a sharecropping basis (*batai*). Nevertheless, some of the ex-tenants-at-will, under-raiyats, etc., have benefited. The Planning Commission states that 3 million of them have become owners (i.e. hold their land directly from the state) of more than 7 million acres as a result of tenancy legislation. However, this is only 2 per cent of the cultivated land of the country. By comparison, the tenants-in-chief of zamindars got title to about 37 per cent of the land of the country. 19·3 per cent of cultivators are still sharecroppers or insecure tenants,[1] and most states refuse to take action to protect them despite prodding from the Central Government, e.g. in West Bengal, zamindari abolition gave land titles to *raiyats*, and tenancy legislation has helped under-raiyats and tenants of under-raiyats, but *bargadars* (share-croppers) get virtually no protection.

In order to prevent excessive resumption of land by ex-zamindars or by other categories of landowner, all states have some kind of ceilings legislation which limits the size of individual holdings. The limit varies from state to state, but generally the area is less than 50 acres. This kind of legislation gets rid of very big landholdings, but there is still great scope for evasion by the middle-size landlord

---

[1] See Planning Commission, *Fourth Five Year Plan, 1969–74*, Delhi, 1970, pp. 176–7. Reliable figures on tenantry are not really available. These Planning Commission figures are from the 1961 census. In view of Daniel Thorner's devastating attack on the 1951 census, 'Agrarian Revolution by Census Redefinition', see D. and A. Thorner, *op. cit.*, Chapter X, they probably understate tenantry.

who predominates in India. The upper limits are fairly generous, the legislation is often not implemented, and holdings can easily be split up amongst family members. By 1970 only 1·1 million acres of land in excess of ceilings had been redistributed by state governments, i.e. less than 0·3 per cent of the land of the country. Landless labourers (who form more than a fifth of the agricultural labour force) have therefore gained very little from all this legislation, except that the abolition of zamindari and jagirdari rights has ended the practice of forced labour (*begar*) and reduced the degree of cringing servility which is required of them.[1] Most of them are outcastes, and none of the land legislation has even seriously considered giving them land.[2] In fact the debates on land reform are full of arguments against helping them.

One of the arguments against change (particularly change involving some degree of expropriation) is that Indian landlords are not Latin American style *latifundistas* but relatively poor people either by world standards, or by comparison with many of India's urban dwellers. This is a reasonable point and is the hub of the problem. Less convincing is the argument that redistribution to the landless would produce uneconomically small holdings and that efficiency would suffer. In Taiwan, there is only a third of the land per member of the labour force as there is in India, its distribution is fairly equal and farm income per head is five times as high as in India. In the long run, a redistribution in which the landless and the sharecroppers acquire title to land may have a substantial beneficial effect on productivity. It is these people who do most of the work on the land in any case, and they would have an incentive to work harder and invest. They would also have more to eat which should raise their productivity.[3] K. N. Raj has argued[4] in the light of economic per-

[1] The biggest improvements in this respect have occurred in some of the old princely states, notably Rajasthan where the old regime was particularly arbitrary and vicious. See G. M. Carstairs, 'A Village in Rajasthan: A Study in Rapid Social Change', in M. N. Srinivas (ed.), *India's Villages*, Asia Publishing House, Bombay, 1969.

[2] Their only real protagonist has been Vinoba Bhave, a former Gandhian politician who has led a crusade for voluntary land gifts (*bhoodan*). However, most landlords who have contributed to this scheme have given waste land. Distribution of bhoodan gifts so far amount to less than 0·5 per cent of the cultivated area.

[3] The average Indian male aged 25–9 weighs only 106 lb., and the average must be well below this for landless labourers. This is less than two-thirds the size of people in prosperous Western countries or in Latin America. See President's Science Advisory Committee, *The World Food Problem*, The White House, Washington, 1967, Vol. II, pp. 39–40. Indian peasants have much less haemoglobin in their blood than Europeans. Any meaningful production function

formance in Japanese and Taiwanese agriculture that a land reform which fixed an upper ceiling of 5 acres on a family holding (except in arid regions) would improve both productivity and social justice. A land reform on this scale would revolutionize the structure of village society and break the economic basis of the caste system. It would also rouse political opposition, and would result in widespread violence in rural areas because it would undoubtedly contain a substantial element of confiscation. However, these costs of transition will probably have to be paid sooner or later, because there is no alternative to land reform if the bottom half of the rural population are to get any benefit at all from economic growth. It is difficult to believe that the costs of transition to a more egalitarian distribution of landownership would be as big as the cost of collectivization in Russia or land reform in Mexico. There would presumably be some kind of financial compensation in India, and deliberate sabotage could not substantially reduce production capacity (as in Russia in 1928–32) simply because there is so little in the way of investment or useful livestock which could be destroyed by the disgruntled losers.

Table VI-2 shows the distribution of landownership in 1953 which apparently has not changed since.[1] There are four main social groups in the countryside. The bottom 23 per cent are those who are landless and destitute. The next 38 per cent have less than 2·5 acres, which is probably the minimum size holding required to provide a subsistence income. The next 26 per cent have economic size holdings, and the top 13 per cent are the village capitalists who have 65 per cent of the land. The village hierarchy remains more or less what it was in the Moghul period. It is not as sharply polarized as in Latin America and the group of rural property owners is large enough to form an effective opposition to social change.

It is clear that Indian land legislation has not established a socialist pattern in agriculture, nor has it upset the hierarchy of caste privilege in village society. It has been a move towards capitalism, with a widening of income differentials between the village capitalists and the landless. The rural structure is still like an onion with many layers. The British peeled off one layer. Zamindar abolition peeled off another. This time, as under the British, all the benefits have been

---

for Indian agriculture must therefore take into account the impact of nutrition on working capacity.

[4] See K. N. Raj, 'Indian Planning: Outline of a Critique and An Alternative Approach' in State Planning Board, *Alternate Policies for the Fourth Five Year Plan*, Kerala, 1969.

[1] See *Report of the Committee on Distribution of Income and Levels of Living*, Part I, Delhi, 1964, pp. 20 and 82.

absorbed by the next two or three layers. These people are less parasitic than the zamindars or the Moghul nobility. Some of them have become capitalist landlords, interested in improving productivity, and others are cultivating peasants with similar aims. But the share-croppers and labourers are still squeezed to a sub-human margin of subsistence as they were under the Moghuls. They know that any increase in their productivity will be siphoned off by others. The system now provides more incentive to increase output than it did before, but less than that of most other countries.

Table VI-2

Distribution of Land-Ownership in India in 1953

Size range of family holding (acres)	Percentage of rural households	Percentage of area
no land	23·09	0·00
0·01–0·99	24·17	1·37
1·00–2·49	13·98	4·86
2·50–4·99	13·49	10·09
5·00–9·99	12·50	18·40
10·00–24·99	9·17	29·11
25·00–49·99	2·66	18·63
50·00 and above	0·94	17·54

Source: Cabinet Secretariat, *National Sample Survey*, Eighth Round, July 1954–April 1955, No. 30, *Report on Land Holdings* (2), Delhi, 1960, p. 7. Ownership is defined as including leased land held under permanent or heritable rights with or without the right to transfer such title. The table therefore understates the degree of inequality in land-ownership. The estimate covers 63·5 million holdings and 305·4 million acres of land.

In the period since independence the growth of farm output has accelerated considerably. From 1948 to 1969, output grew by 2·3 per cent a year, compared with a mere 0·7 per cent from 1900 to 1946 (see Appendix B). There are several reasons why this happened. In the first place, population growth has accelerated because of the advances in medicine and public health. It is, in fact, rather mysterious why death rates fell as much as they did in Indian conditions,[1] but

[1] Life expectation has risen from thirty to fifty years in the past two decades. The decline in mortality is due to several causes: (a) improved water supply in

106

as a result there has been great pressure to expand the cultivated area. This was made somewhat easier by zamindari reform which released waste land to the state. Between 1948 and 1966 the cultivated area increased by 1·9 per cent a year. Some of the land was of poor quality, but the expansion in area explains a good deal of the growth in output, and the government has also spent a good deal to promote consolidation of scattered holdings. From 1900 to 1946, cultivated area expanded by only 0·5 per cent a year.

The main public effort to help agriculture has been expenditure on irrigation, continuing the British tradition. The irrigated area rose by 2·1 per cent a year from 46·7 million acres in 1948 to 68 million in 1966. Under British rule the irrigated area increased more slowly, by 1·5 per cent a year from 1898 to 1943. Irrigation increases yields, permits double cropping in some areas and helps stabilize output because it increases the certainty of water supply. It is essential for the exploitation of modern technology and the increase of productivity. The total cultivated area in 1966 was 339 million acres, of which only 68 million were irrigated. Most of the irrigation water is sold by state governments at highly subsidized rates.

Since independence the government has taken vigorous steps to improve rural credit. Agricultural credit co-operatives were started by the British in 1904, but the movement was never very big. It has now been greatly extended. The government participates in share capital, helps finance bad debts, gives technical advice and helps with training. Many societies are moribund or have a bad debt recovery experience, but between 1951 and 1968 co-operative credit rose from 3 per cent to a third of total credit used by farmers, and membership of co-ops rose from 5 to 28 million. Co-operatives now distribute about 60 per cent of fertilizer used in agriculture as well as other farm inputs. Outstanding loans in 1969 were Rs. 4·9 billion for short and medium term, and Rs. 1·2 billion long term. Most of this credit goes to people with a clear title to land as they are the only ones who can offer security for loans. It has undoubtedly helped to increase investment and output, but insecure tenants, share-croppers and agricultural labourers have received no benefit from these schemes. They have to rely on the traditional moneylenders

---

both villages and towns. This has substantially reduced the incidence of cholera, typhoid and hepatitis; (b) smallpox vaccination has reduced deaths from this disease to negligible proportions; (c) malaria eradication programmes by D.D.T. spraying have eliminated the disease in very many areas; (d) large-scale sales of new antibiotic drugs have cut the incidence of many diseases; (e) improvements in health services.

whose terms are more expensive than those of co-operatives. Co-operatives are usually run by the locally dominant caste in each area and their operations have been marked by caste and political favouritism. Some of the borrowers from co-operatives are money-lenders who use the credit to help finance their own operations.

The government has taken a number of measures to promote village uplift, some of which have had an impact on output. Community development was started in 1952 as a multi-purpose programme to encourage self-help activities. It was intended to recruit voluntary labour to build roads, wells, schools and health centres, and to incorporate an agricultural extension service. In order to implement the programme the country has been divided into 5,265 blocks, each with a development officer, assisted by a cadre of village-level workers. Altogether the personnel involved in these programmes was about 80,000, compared with about 2,000 in agricultural extension in colonial times. In practice, there is too much conflict of interest within village society to get any significant voluntary effort. The upper castes will not soil their hands with labour or risk physical contact with untouchables, and the latter have little incentive to provide free labour on schemes which are most likely to benefit upper castes. Furthermore, village-level workers were not technically competent to undertake the wide range of activity envisaged and were at too low a level either to enthuse or command[1] any significant activity. The failure of the village uplift programme was already recognized in 1957 in the report of the Balwantrai Mehta Committee. It has been continued *de jure*, but since 1965 the personnel involved have been switched very largely on to agricultural extension work and the Ministry of Community Development has been merged with the Ministry of Food and Agriculture.

Agricultural research has contributed to the growth of output. In the 1960s there was a technological breakthrough in the use of new seeds, particularly new Mexican strains of wheat. These can only be used in the limited areas where there is suitable irrigation, and their impact has therefore been highly concentrated in Punjab, Gujarat and Madras. The catastrophic 1965 and 1966 harvests had a useful cathartic effect in highlighting the urgency of government action. However, the basic ignorance of the rural population and its

[1] The programme did have antecedents, e.g. the work of F. L. Brayne, a British administrator in the Punjab in the 1920s, but Brayne was a much more powerful and enthusiastic figure than any village-level worker or block development officer, and he was working in a more restricted area. The same is true of the work of Albert Mayer, the American enthusiast for community development who ran a project at Etawah with help from the Ford Foundation which was the precursor of the 1952 scheme.

lack of education make progress difficult and in livestock husbandry religious beliefs are an additional barrier.

Since independence, the incentives for private investment in agriculture have increased, (a) because farmers have better titles to their land, (b) because there are better credit facilities, and (c) because there are new technical possibilities. Tubewells and pumps are now available, and government programmes have brought electricity to about a sixth of the villages, compared with about ½ per cent at independence. There has, therefore, been a big increase in private irrigation. In 1950 there were only 3,500 tubewells, compared with 376,000 in 1969. Growth in fertilizer consumption was held up for a time by the inefficiency of industrial policy, but by 1969 consumption of nitrogenous fertilizer was 1·4 million tons, compared with 56,000 tons in 1950.

The tax burden on agriculture has declined steadily since independence. Farmers are not subject to the general income tax, and the derisory agricultural income tax which some states levy is paid almost entirely by plantations. Land tax is not progressive and amounts to only 0·8 per cent of farm income. The higher incomes in agriculture remain virtually untaxed. With the new agricultural technology, the relatively favourable prices of fertilizers and tractors and high taxes outside farming, agriculture is becoming a more attractive proposition for urban capitalists, and mechanized farming is spreading, particularly in areas near big cities which provide ready markets.

Mechanized farming is hardly a desirable prospect in India, which has so much surplus labour and so little capital. The agricultural sector has very large scope for exploiting labour-intensive techniques. India should therefore be moving its agriculture towards the Japanese–Taiwanese model of labour-intensive midget farms for efficiency reasons as well as to promote social justice.

Since 1953 the Indian government has received a large amount of surplus U.S. food more or less free under Public Law 480 ($3·3 billion worth from 1953 to 1966). This food was sold by the government in urban areas and kept prices lower than they would otherwise have been. This naturally had a discouraging effect on production incentives.[1] Government policies to restrict the internal trade in food have

[1] See N. Rath and V. S. Patvardhan, *Impact of Assistance Under P.L. 480 on Indian Economy*, Asia Publishing House, London, 1967, p. 200: 'While inflationary pressures have pushed the general price level steadily upwards, the Government with the help of P.L. 480 imports had tried to hold the price of wheat at an artificially low, unchanging level all through. It has meant steady lowering of the price of wheat. . . . The Government has apparently never seriously considered the fact that at least part of the burden of its price policy

had the same effect. Because of food shortage the country had been split into food zones between which private trade was not permitted. This increased production incentives in areas of deficit, but reduced them in areas of surplus and thus reduced regional specialization and productivity. In 1965 (when bad weather reduced output by 12 per cent) farm prices rose substantially, and the price situation has since remained more favourable to farmers than it was before 1965. The government now adds to its stocks of grain in years of good harvest (like 1967) to provide price support, and in 1965 created the Food Corporation of India which has added considerably to official storage facilities.

Agricultural performance has varied widely between states. In the past two decades output grew by more than 4 per cent a year in Punjab, Gujarat and Madras, but in West Bengal, Uttar Pradesh and Assam it rose by less than 2 per cent a year. There has been no relationship between productive performance and the changes in land tenure. Changes in land tenure have been minimal in Punjab and Madras. The real advantage of the fast-growing states has been the availability of reliable irrigation water which is essential for the exploitation of the new agricultural technology.

Since independence there has been an increase in farm income per person in agriculture, but the magnitude has been difficult to measure because of statistical problems concerning output, employment and relative prices. The increase has probably been between 0·5 and 1 per cent a year in real terms. However, all this has gone to people who own land, i.e. rentiers, working proprietors and higher-caste tenants. Landless labourers and sharecroppers have probably had no gain in real income since independence, because they have nothing to sell but their labour and they are operating in a situation where labour is abundant and they have no bargaining power. There is no mechanism by which the benefits of economic growth are filtered down (as is so often assumed in the plan).

The only government effort directed mainly at the interests of the poorest section of the rural population, is the Works Programme. This is a scheme for labour-intensive public works. It was intended in the Third Plan to provide 2·5 million people with about 100 days employment during the slack agricultural season. However, the scheme did not acquire momentum and only 400,000 people were employed. This represents about 0·1 million man-years of employment, which is hardly significant for the landless labourers who

and the resource for development, is being borne by the farmer, chiefly the wheat farmer in India. The lowering of the price of wheat results in adverse terms of trade, which is like a tax on the farmer.'

number 40 million. The Fourth Plan talks of the continuation of a token works programme, but with no conviction of its effectiveness.

If the bottom half of the rural population are to receive any benefit from the general acceleration of economic growth, they must be able to acquire land. Unfortunately, agricultural taxation and land tenure legislation are not within the constitutional competence of the Central government, but lie in the hands of the seventeen states, and for this reason alone progress would be slow, apart from the vested interest of the larger farmers. However, there seems no doubt about the pattern of change which is desirable, and there may be some scope for pushing state governments into action through fiscal policy as follows:[1]

(a) abolition of land tax on holdings under 2 acres, and heavily progressive taxation above that level, rising to 30 per cent of gross product above 25 acres;

(b) creation of a Land Bank to purchase land from bigger peasants and to sell only to peasants holding less than 2 acres. Payment to be made on the instalment plan;

(c) a 10 per cent tax on all sales of agricultural land, where the purchaser is not the Land Bank or a peasant holding less than 2 acres;

(d) withholding Centre contributions to state budgets to the extent that they do not increase land tax.

6. *Industry*

By the mid-1950s it was clear that the social changes brought by independence were not very significant. Princes and zamindars had become state pensioners, significant land reform was blocked, and it was obvious that the programmes for community development and co-operation would have little social impact. Nehru therefore launched an offensive for 'socialism' in the industrial sector.

In December 1954, parliament was persuaded to adopt a resolution accepting the goal of a 'socialist pattern of society', and in 1955 the Avadi session of the Congress party endorsed the idea of a large public sector.

The second plan was the main vehicle for formulating the socialist strategy. At this period Nehru was a very active Chairman of the Planning Commission, which had been set up in 1950 but which really blossomed about 1954. The Planning Commission was to some extent Nehru's personal secretariat, an enclave of special loyalty

---

[1] A scheme for progressive land taxation is outlined by I.M.D. Little, 'Tax Policy and the Third Plan', in P. N. Rosenstein-Rodan, *Pricing and Fiscal Policies*, Allen and Unwin, London, 1964.

within the bureaucratic hierarchy. By comparison the Finance Ministry was conservative. From 1950 to 1956 the Minister was C. D. Deshmukh, an ex-member of the I.C.S. who has since become a leader of the Swatantra party. Nehru's main collaborator in the Planning Commission was Professor P. C. Mahalanobis, the head of the Indian Statistical Institute, who shared Nehru's enthusiasm for the Soviet model of development and Soviet planning techniques, and who was a corresponding member of the Soviet Academy of Sciences.

The major aim of the socialist strategy was to increase the size of the public sector rapidly. The life insurance companies and the Imperial Bank of India were nationalized in 1956, but private industrial enterprises were not nationalized as many of the leading industrialists were financial supporters of Congress. However, the public sector was to grow 'both absolutely and in comparison and at a faster rate than the private sector'. In the long run this might lead to a complete state takeover, but this was left vague and was not an essential part of the doctrine. The policy did not challenge the basic property rights of capitalists, but limited the area in which they operated. The new dispensation would reduce the scope for accumulation of wealth and large incomes in private hands. It was intended to curb monopolies. There was little hesitation in defining which sectors should be in the public domain. It was taken as axiomatic that certain industries were 'commanding heights' which would enable the government to exercise 'countervailing power'. It was also argued that Indian capitalism was too weak to develop some 'essential' industries. The Industrial Policy Resolution of 1956 put it as follows: 'all industries of basic and strategic importance, or in the nature of public utility services, should be in the public sector. Other industries which are essential and require investment on a scale which only the State in present circumstances could provide, have also to be in the public sector.' The latter point was an exaggeration as there were already some very big firms in the private sector, some of which, Tata and I.I.S.C., owned steel mills and another, Birla, had wanted to build one.

In fact, the word 'pattern' was more important than the word 'socialist'. There was a general feeling, bolstered by the work of popular nationalist historians like R. C. Dutt and Nehru, and Marxists like Palme Dutt, that colonialism had left India with an industrial structure inappropriate in two respects. In the first place heavy industry had been neglected. It was felt that India's size and her rich endowment of iron ore and coal warranted a big expansion in the steel industry, as well as the creation of atomic energy plants and heavy industry. Secondly, it was felt, particularly by the Gandhians, that colonialism had destroyed handicrafts and that these should be revived. It was argued strongly that this would create more employment than any other pattern. Here as in the historical literature on India's de-industrialization, the plan presented no professional analysis of the costs and benefits of 'handicrafts' versus machine products, and the income creating, productivity raising aspects of modern technology were not discussed. The Mahalanobis proposals were, therefore, a curious amalgam of Stalinist and Ruskinian views, with large investments in heavy industry, and substantial investment and subsidies for handicrafts. Manufactured consumer goods were to be taxed where they competed with handicrafts, and were to get very little in the way of investment. He proposed to allocate 79 per cent of industrial investment to heavy industry, 14 per cent to handicrafts and only 7 per cent to consumer goods.

The other important aspect of the socialist *pattern* was the emphasis on self-sufficiency. Here again the rationale was eclectic. It derived partly from the nationalist swadeshi movement which had boycotted foreign goods from 1905 onwards and was elaborated by Gandhi into a mystique emphasizing the holy quality of Indian products.[1] To some degree it represented unnecessary mimicry of the Soviet pattern of 1928–33 which, by the compulsions of international politics and the business cycle, had had to be autarchic to a degree inappropriate in India. Some preference for autarchy was legitimate in view of India's past experience in two World Wars and in the Korean war when her access to foreign capital goods was cut off. The temporary U.S. embargo on weapon supply in 1965 was a further demonstration of the need for reasonable self-sufficiency in military lines. But the argument for an extreme degree of import substitution was also based on a profound pessimism about exports. 'A country which seeks rapid development cannot rely on the export of food and raw materials for satisfying the major part of its increasing requirements of capital goods. Nor can a comparative late comer in the field of industrialization hope for a sizeable expansion in the exports of manufactured consumer goods.'[2] There was no reference to the impact of the exchange rate on exports, though the rupee had been substantially overvalued since 1925.

[1] 'If not an article of commerce had not been brought from outside India, she would today be a land flowing with milk and honey,' M. K. Gandhi, *The Gospel of Swadeshi*, Bharatiya Vidya Bhavan, Bombay, 1967.
[2] Planning Commission, *Papers Relating to the Formulation of the Second Five Year Plan*, Delhi, 1955, p. 76.

113

The government encouraged public discussion of the Mahalanobis 'plan-frame'. There was not as much time to explore alternatives as in the Soviet industrialization debates in the 'twenties between Preobrazhensky and Bukharin. However, Vakil and Brahmananda did make fundamental criticisms and suggest something more like a Japanese strategy with more emphasis on agriculture. K. N. Raj suggested a bolder model with more emphasis on consumption. The Gokhale Institute questioned the usefulness of the emphasis on handicrafts.[1]

The most fundamental problem in justifying the Mahalanobis strategy (or in postulating interventionist alternatives) was the lack of any reliable statistics on demand. In the first place it turned out that population growth in the second plan period was about 2·1 per cent a year instead of 1·2 per cent as he assumed. Secondly, there were no reliable figures on income distribution or elasticities of demand. Mahalanobis had to work simply with figures on production and trade, and crude capital–output ratios. He did not have the elaborate input–output data and material balances which later emerged from the Planning Commission. Technically he was less well equipped than Strumilin, Stalin's main architect for the 1928 plan. He had a further disadvantage compared to Strumilin, that he was not an economist. His was mainly an investment plan rather than an analysis of the way the economy normally worked and how his proposals would change the pattern of consumer satisfaction. Although the arguments for small-scale industry were based on the idea that they would create employment, nothing much was known about the problem, and the Fourth Plan fifteen years later acknowledged this by dropping any statistical estimates of employment and unemployment. Furthermore, the statistics on investment in the private sector were very poor. As K. N. Raj said at the time, investment estimates were 'largely shots in the dark and can, at best, indicate only the broad orders of magnitude'. It was clear from the very beginning that India would not and could not[2] mount an effort at resource mobilization on the Soviet scale. At the time much of the discussion of this point was concerned with the dangers of

[1] See Panel of Economists, *Papers Relating to the Formulation of the Second Five Year Plan*, Planning Commission, Delhi, 1955.

[2] India could doubtless have mobilized more resources for investment by a bolder fiscal policy, but her capacity to squeeze savings out of the mass of the population was limited because so many lived on the verge of subsistence. In 1955 Indian *per capita* food consumption was only a third of that in the U.S.S.R. in 1928: see A. Maddison, *Economic Growth in Japan and the U.S.S.R.*, Norton, New York, 1969, pp. 161–2, and A. Maddison, *Economic Progress and Policy in Developing Countries*, p. 287.

inflation and price increases but there was inadequate appreciation of the very obvious risk of surplus capacity because the demand pattern could not be made to match the forecast.

Another major characteristic of the Indian economy which was ignored was its instability. Because of the severity of harvest fluctuations, and the size of agriculture in the economy, it is inevitable that the economy will be more unstable than that of most countries even with efficient short-term economic policy. Given the shortage of foreign exchange, low level of government food stocks, and the inelasticity of the fiscal system, the cushions for instability were small. It was, therefore, risky to embark on a growth pattern in which an appreciable amount of resources, particularly foreign exchange resources, were tied up in projects with an eight-year gestation period. There was some virtue in remaining dependent on imports for some of the goods for which demand is most volatile.

The Second Plan was a modified version of the Mahalanobis plan-frame, with heavy emphasis on steel and capital goods, and considerable favours to small-scale industry, but with a bigger scope than Mahalanobis had proposed for consumer goods. In fact economic performance was somewhat different from what was expected. Private consumption and the private manufacture of consumer goods expanded more quickly than was expected. This caused a balance of payments crisis in 1958 and led to much tighter import controls, which impeded efficiency. But the payments crisis also led to more foreign aid, and its net impact was probably helpful. The new investments in heavy industry proved slower in gestation than had been expected because of technical and managerial problems, 1960–1 output from the three new steel plants was 0·6 million instead of 2 million tons. The fertilizer plants were more than a year late. Heavy machinery, mining machinery and foundry/forge projects were still in their initial stages. However, 1960 national income was 20 per cent higher than in 1955. This was lower than the 25 per cent growth target, but it was somewhat better than the 18 per cent achieved in the First Plan from 1950–5.

The Third Plan strategy (for 1960–5) was similar to that of the Second (for 1955–60). But the growth target was now 30 per cent instead of 25 per cent, partly because it was realized that population growth was much faster than had been supposed in making the Second Plan. During the first four years of the Third Plan, the economy grew a little faster than in the Second Plan, but 1965 was a catastrophic year in which the economy was struck by three severe blows which had nothing to do with economic policy. The most important was a drought which produced a fall in farm output bigger than any since 1920, and necessitated large imports of food. The second was the war with Pakistan which itself did negligible damage, but escalated military expenditure and military imports which had already been doubled since the 1962 border war with China. The third was the temporary cessation and subsequent levelling out of U.S. aid, which had previously grown steadily since 1958. The drop in agricultural output and the sharp rise in food prices led to a fall in demand for industrial consumer goods and to a fall in private industrial investment. These movements reduced private demand for the products of state industry, and the government accentuated the recession by cutting public investment (a) because its tax receipts had fallen substantially, (b) because the cut in aid and the high level of food imports had put a sharp strain on foreign exchange availability, (c) because it began to dawn on the administration that its policy for industrial resource allocation involved strategic error, and (d) because some old-fashioned people in the Finance Ministry were worried that government spending would cause prices to rise faster. As a result, national income fell about 5·5 per cent in 1965, and the net growth of national income in the Third Plan period was only 13 per cent instead of the 30 per cent projected. In 1965, steel output was 4·5 million tons instead of the 6·8 million target. Because of this crisis situation the Fourth Plan was postponed and the government switched the emphasis to *ad hoc* one-year plans.

In 1966 the harvest was as bad as in 1965 and there was virtually no rise in national income. In 1967 national income rebounded with the recovery of agriculture. In 1968 it stagnated again. In 1969 it increased by over 5 per cent, but 1969 output per head was still below 1964 levels and only 6·6 per cent higher than in 1960. The 1965–6 recession was due to forces beyond the control of economic policy, but its extreme severity and the poor recovery record also reflects faults of policy. In 1969, many capital goods industries were working well below capacity even though capacity itself was well below that which was intended. In some cases low output was due to almost total lack of demand. The worst cases were the industries producing capital goods for heavy industry. In 1968 the government plant making heavy machine tools was working at 3 per cent capacity, the foundry and forge at 7 per cent and heavy machine building at 13 per cent. The Mining and Allied Machinery Company worked at 6 per cent of capacity. These are cases in which government built the wrong plants. In steel and fertilizer, there was demand and capacity, but low production. Here implementation, not strategy, was at fault.

Looking back, it seems that the 'socialist pattern' involved too much emphasis on heavy industry and not enough on consumer goods industries or agriculture. A greater emphasis on consumer goods and agriculture would have left the economy more flexible, permitted faster growth, and would have made exports easier. The Fourth Plan which was finally approved in 1970 shows some move in this direction.

The economic difficulties which have arisen from the 'socialist pattern' are not simply due to choice of the wrong product mix, but to the inefficient way state enterprises have been run. Several countries run a successful mixed economy with a large public sector. In Brazil, France and Mexico, there is a close symbiosis between private and public activity in terms of finance, technical co-operation, transfer of managerial personnel, and joint planning of investments. But, in India, the sharp segregation of the two sectors has been harmful. The government prevented private industrialists (both home and foreign) from expanding in fields in which they had the necessary technical and managerial resources and where those of government were stretched to breaking point, and it also failed to recruit enough managers from the private sector for state plants. Only recently has it embarked on joint projects with the private sector.

In steel, in which government has invested Rs. 13 billion, it would have been cheaper to expand existing capacity in the private sector and to have built two instead of three completely new steel plants in the public sector. In 1968 the Tata steel works (private) were producing at 90 per cent capacity, whereas the figure in the public sector was 60 per cent. Tata made profits. The government made losses. It took about four decades before the Tata Company was able to Indianize its top management completely, and it was obviously unwise not to use these talents more fully. If it had not been for official controls, the private sector would have expanded capacity to some extent from the early 1950s onwards, but it was only in the 1960s, when it was apparent that the official plan targets would not be met, that the private sector was allowed to expand. The same is also true of the fertilizer industry. Government progress with fertilizers was slow, at a time when foreign investors were being discouraged from investment in this industry. In 1965, government plants produced 230,000 tons of nitrogenous fertilizer when the target was over 800,000 tons.

State enterprises are inefficient for several reasons. One reason is that the top managers are civil servants without industrial experience. In the steel industry 'decisions about promotions and dismissals, spare parts and replacements, and a number of other matters, some extraordinarily trivial' are delayed by the bureaucratic reluctance to take responsibility. 'The general manager and his subordinates frequently had a distinguished record with a state or central ministry. Often the general manager was nearing retirement or was brought out of retirement to manage the plant. Thus, Rourkela has had seven general managers in about as many years; Bhilai and Durgapur have each had four. Some plant officials have regarded their tenure at the plant as way stations in their careers not to be tarnished by a wrong decision.'[1] Personnel policy for management was even less imaginative than in the U.K. in the 1950s, to say nothing about comparison with Mattei in Italy, Dreyfus in France, or the people who run nationalized plants in Mexico and Brazil.

Even if managers were highly skilled they would be handicapped because they are ultimately responsible to parliament, which is not the case in other countries with a large public sector like France, Italy or the U.K. This practice has led to inefficiency:

'It is generally agreed that a public enterprise, if it is to be run successfully, must possess a sufficient degree of autonomy from Government and Parliament. When day-to-day decisions of a public enterprise become the subject of parliamentary inter-pellations and discussions, the Ministers find it necessary to ask for advance knowledge and approval of all decisions. Moreover, exposed to constant public scrutiny, the management will be afraid of making the day-to-day decisions necessary in commercial undertakings, and an ostensibly autonomous enterprise will be virtually stifled by red tape and bureaucracy.'[2]

There has recently been some improvement in auditing procedures to gear them to the needs of modern business, but senior managers are constantly inundated with demands for favours (jobs for nephews, etc.) backed by blackmailing threats to make political trouble. Finally, managers are badly paid. The upper salary has been Rs. 2,500 a month (about $4,000 a year) which does not compete with the private sector and is not much for managing assets worth several hundred million dollars.

Public enterprise is also handicapped by high labour costs. Wages in public enterprises were set initially at a high level, and perquisites were universal in the form of heavily subsidized housing. The number of people engaged was excessive, and unions have concentrated their wage demands and strikes on state plants because they know that they are the most likely place to win concessions.

Because of delays in construction, misjudgement of demand

[1] See W. A. Johnson, *The Steel Industry of India*, Oxford University Press, 1967.
[2] See Planning Commission, *The Third Five Year Plan*, Delhi, 1965, p. 268.

patterns, mistakes in price policy, managerial and labour difficulties, major parts of the state sector have made heavy losses. Net losses after allowing for depreciation, interest and taxes averaged 0·4 per cent a year on capital employed from 1965 to 1969. The only year in the quinquennium when there was a positive net profit was 1965. The losses have been concentrated on steel, heavy engineering, mining machinery and heavy electricals. Overall, the public industrial sector has made no contribution to financing the growth of the economy. By 1968 public investment in industry was about Rs. 39 billion, i.e. about a third of industrial assets in the organized sector (compared with 2 per cent in 1950), but output was only about a tenth of that in the organized sector, and employment was about one-sixth (757,000 in March 1969).

We must therefore conclude that the government's industrial strategy hindered economic growth, firstly, because of mistakes in the pattern chosen—particularly the emphasis on machines to make machines, and the neglect of exports. The common accusation that agriculture was neglected is somewhat exaggerated because agriculture's performance was so deeply affected by bad weather. Secondly, the implementation of the public sector programme was very inefficient, but has proved difficult to remedy. And, thirdly, and perhaps most fundamental, it is difficult to see what the new pattern has done to promote equality of income and social mobility, or in what sense it has really damaged the interests of Indian capitalists. It might be argued that the protection to small-scale industry and handicrafts has been beneficial, but employment gains have been offset by inefficiency, waste of capital and poor quality products. If the main goal were to promote employment it seems extraordinary to have put so much emphasis on capital intensive projects in the state sector.

The socialist pattern of industrialization involves a large amount of control over the activity of the private sector of industry, which still produces 90 per cent of output in the organized sector. Entry to or expansion of certain lines of activity is regulated by the Industrial Policy Resolutions of 1948 and 1956. The Resolution of 1948 reserved munitions, atomic energy and railways entirely for government, as well as new ventures in coal, iron, steel, aircraft, shipbuilding, telegraph and telephone materials and minerals. The 1956 Resolution specified two schedules, in the first of which the state would normally take responsibility for expanding output in its own plants. The seventeen items specified included the nine listed in 1948, plus heavy plant and machinery, air transport and electricity distribution. The second schedule listed industries in which new developments were expected both by the state and private sector. There were twelve of these including machine tools, chemicals, fertilizers and antibiotics, road and sea transport. The rest of industry was to be the sphere of the private sector.

The basic instrument for controlling private industry was the Industries (Development and Regulation) Act 1951. Thirty-seven industries were specified, covering almost all of manufacturing, mining and power. Firms were required to register with the government and seek licences for expansion of capacity. In addition the government controlled allocations and prices of raw materials and capital goods, and could also control the price of the final product. These licensing powers were reinforced by controls over capital issues and foreign exchange. All imported raw materials and capital were very closely controlled. The degree of control was thus much greater than that of any 'mixed' economy in the Western world in peacetime conditions. The closest parallel was the British economy in the years 1945–9 before Harold Wilson introduced his bonfire of controls. Some developing countries have attempted to work equally detailed schemes of control, but they have never succeeded for very long because it put too great a strain on their administrative capacity. Even communist countries have felt the conflict between controls and efficiency. In the U.S.S.R., Liberman has proclaimed the virtues of the price mechanism, and in Hungary and Yugoslavia de-control has got to a stage where managers of communist state enterprises are freer than capitalist entrepreneurs in the private sector in India.

Detailed regulation was intended to serve several purposes. The first was to secure a pattern of development in 'the public interest', as opposed to one determined by market forces. Market forces were regarded with particular distrust because unfettered capitalism was associated with colonialism and the pre-war record of capitalism in securing economic growth was not impressive. There was strong official support for handicraft and small-scale industry which needed protection against market forces. There was also a feeling that inessential luxury good consumption needed to be controlled via production. In this respect controls were intended to offset weaknesses in fiscal policy. Furthermore it was claimed that controls would prevent monopoly, and could contribute to balanced regional development.

By the early 1960s it was obvious that the inordinately detailed controls over the private sector were creating considerable inefficiency:

'Detailed controls not only put considerable strain on the administrative machinery, but led to delayed implementation.

Further the controls did not always secure the objectives for which they were designed. The system of controls also resulted in private enterprise becoming increasingly dependent on Government and ceasing to carry out its own entrepreneurial functions, including market studies. Another serious shortcoming which characterized the activities of the private sector was inadequate cost-consciousness and little appreciation of the essential need to reduce such costs, because of the existence of a sellers' market.'[1]

The best evidence of administrative strain was the long delay in awarding licences. The Mathur Committee cited cases of eighteen month delays for import licences.[2] The Raj Committee showed the dangers in official allocation of resources whose market value was above their controlled price.[3] In this situation there are important windfall gains to the lucky recipients, some black marketeering, and official corruption. Licences are based on the traditional share of the market or production capacity, and the Dutt report found that the system had a strong bias in favour of the 'larger industrial houses',[4] whose monopolistic privileges it was supposed to limit.

As a result of this evidence official faith in detailed controls has waned. Sixteen commodities were freed from price and distribution control in 1963, and controls on several other industries, such as iron and steel, coal, fertilizers and commercial vehicles were relaxed. Sugar has been partially de-controlled, price control in paper has been lifted. The private sector has been given greater freedom to expand capacity. In 1964 the exemption limit for licensing of new assets was raised from Rs. 1 million to Rs. 2·5 million, and licensing provisions were relaxed.

Between 1965 and 1969 there was extensive re-examination of the control mechanism which culminated in the proposals laid down in the Fourth Five Year Plan. This reflects a fundamental preference for controls, but their extent is to be limited to large firms largely for pragmatic reasons.

In the first place, there is now a list of 'core' industries which are 'basic, essential, and strategic'. These include equipment and fertilizers for agriculture, iron and steel, non-ferrous metals, petroleum

---

[1] See Planning Commission, *Fourth Five Year Plan 1969–74*, Delhi, 1970, p. 302.

[2] See Government of India, *Report of the Study Team on Import and Export Trade Control Organization*, New Delhi, 1965.

[3] See Ministry of Steel and Heavy Industries, *Report on Steel Control*, New Delhi, October 1963, which pointed out the extensive licence applications by bogus importers.

[4] See Ministry of Industrial Development, *Report of Industrial Licensing Policy Committee* (Main Report), New Delhi, July 1969.

and its products, coking coal, heavy machinery, shipbuilding, newsprint and electronics. In these fields, targets, priorities and controls will be applied. Firms investing more than Rs. 10 million will also be subject to investment licensing as will all investments by the twenty biggest firms and by all foreign firms. Firms investing below Rs. 10 million will be free from control and the plan will not set targets and priorities for their output. For fifty-five items the right to expand production will be reserved for small-scale industry, and twenty big monopoly companies will be restrained from expansion outside 'core' industries. All foreign exchange will be licensed. The recent Monopolies Act and the nationalization of fourteen Commercial Banks are also intended as measures to restrain the activities of the twenty largest firms.

There is no doubt that these reductions in controls will help efficiency, but too many of them still remain. Thus, firms whose economic performance is poor will still get a guarantee against bankruptcy and an income which is really a government subsidy rather than a reward for enterprise. The sufferers are the mass of the people who, as consumers, get poorer quality goods at higher prices than if there were competition, and small entrepreneurs who are kept out of certain lines of business or cannot expand because they cannot get credit, supplies of scarce domestic materials, or imports.

We may therefore ask why there is such reluctance to end a system which reduces economic growth and enhances inequality. The main reason is vested interest. In business circles, the large firms and those which are well established actually like controls because they reduce risks and guarantee profits. Competition is not a well-established part of the business ethic. Controls are useful to bureaucrats because they enlarge their career prospects, increase their power and prestige, and provide some of them with an illegitimate source of income. De-control would also reveal past bureaucratic error. For these reasons, the Administrative Reforms Commission is full of double talk about controls. There is a clear acknowledgement of their damaging effect, but a fear of living without them: 'The working of the market forces cannot be relied upon to discourage the demands of sectors which are considered less essential from the point of view of the Plan or to automatically meet the needs of those sectors which are essential to planned development. Low priority activities could be quite capable of yielding high profits and the free play of market forces could render certain essential activities commercially less attractive than the low priority ones. It will, therefore, be necessary to take positive action for channelling the resources towards high priority activities by means of physical controls. The import control mechanism is also rendered necessary by the heterogeneous nature and inconvertibility of the large portion of India's foreign resources. Having committed the country's capital to industries considered to be of high priority, we can afford neither to starve them of their imported input requirements nor leave them at the mercy of the price mechanism.'[1] Later on they reject the idea that import licences might be auctioned. This, of course, would be bringing in the price mechanism by the back door. It is remarkable that there should still be such staggering confidence in the capacity of the bureaucracy to judge the public interest considering the acknowledged failures in the past.

The ultimate argument of the 'control-wallahs' is the theory that imports are a specially scarce resource which only the government can allocate in the interests of the nation. However, the main reason why imports are so desirable is that the government sells them so cheaply. The exchange rate greatly overvalues the rupee, so that people getting import licences are really getting a large subsidy. The government uses a lot of imports for the public sector, but here, too, resources are used wastefully because the price of goods understates their real value. The overvaluation of the exchange rate in itself is a major cause of the payments problem because it harms exports. India's export performance has been very poor. Manufactured exports have performed worse than those of practically any other country: even quite small countries like Hong Kong, Korea and Taiwan have bigger manufactured exports than India. The devaluation of 1966 did do something to alleviate the inefficiency of this system, but there had previously been a number of export incentives which were abolished, and new export duties were imposed on some exports which were previously competitive, so the net effect of devaluation was small. Now some of the earlier export incentives have been restored, but the $4\frac{1}{2}$ rupee differential between the black market rate (12 rupees to the dollar) and the official rate (7·5 rupees to the dollar) is an indication that overvaluation persists. The official argument that the black market in currency is marginal and therefore not representative is not very impressive. It was generally acknowledged by Indian nationalists that the Indian currency was overvalued when the silver standard was abandoned after 1898, and that it was even more overvalued in the inter-war years. However, the rupee was kept at its 1925 parity with sterling until 1966 in spite of greater price increases in India. It would in fact seem desirable to make a move towards a floating exchange rate, at least for private

[1] Administrative Reforms Commission, *Report on Economic Administration*, Delhi, July 1968, pp. 39–40.

transactions. This would improve efficiency considerably and remove much of the rationale for controls.

Apart from import controls, which have increased the power of domestic industry to exploit consumers, the Tariff Commission has shown willingness to protect any domestic industry physically capable of competing with imports. However, since the payments crisis of 1958 when India exhausted its surplus foreign exchange reserves, industry has hardly needed tariff protection as there have been tight quantitative restrictions on practically all imports.

There are several ways in which government activity has favoured private industrialists in ways that amount to subsidization. The government has taken more or less full responsibility for 'infra-structure' investment, which has been an even bigger burden than investment in state industrial enterprises. The railways have been expensively re-equipped and the electricity network greatly enlarged. These government services have generally been sold at prices lower than a commercial enterprise would have charged, as is also true of products like steel and capital equipment manufactured by state plants.

There are government development banks which have provided favoured sectors of private industry with loans at relatively low interest rates. There has been a finance corporation at the centre and in each state, and in 1964 the Industrial Development Bank was set up to augment and co-ordinate existing activities. The Unit Trust of India was set up in 1964 to channel savings towards risk capital. The State Life Insurance Corporation also invests in the private sector. In 1969 the government nationalized fourteen commercial banks which were linked to some of the biggest private industrial groups, and in future the resources of these banks should be made available to smaller firms, though a good deal will no doubt be directed towards the public sector at unrealistically low interest rates.

Another way in which Indian capitalists have been helped is by the various restrictions on foreign private investment. As a result, India's *per capita* receipts of foreign capital have been smaller than those of almost any other country (only $0·20 *per capita* annual average from 1960 to 1965, compared with $0·60 for Pakistan, $3·10 for the Philippines, $2·70 for South Korea, $2·30 for Taiwan, and $2.70 for Thailand). Many old British firms have disinvested capital, and the relative share of foreigners in industry has declined considerably. Foreign firms are now under strong pressure to hire Indian managerial personnel to train them and upgrade them quickly, so the situation has changed considerably since the colonial period. There have also been reforms in the managing agency system (the

Indian Companies Amendment Act) which have reduced the monopolistic power of foreign firms, and they no longer enjoy favoured status *vis-à-vis* government. The number of managing agencies has dropped considerably, but monopolistic holdings have simply taken new forms.

The government has spent a good deal on industrial research. By 1969 expenditure on scientific research and development had risen to 0·4 per cent of national income and 94 per cent of this was financed by the government. The total scientific and technical manpower engaged on R and D was about 62,000 in 1968. This expenditure has added to India's technical capacity, but about 40 per cent has gone into nuclear energy projects which have little economic and no social justification and must be regarded primarily as a military outlay. In 1966–9 the Council of Scientific and Industrial Research sponsored projects costing Rs. 546 million, the Department of Atomic Energy Rs. 566 million and the Ministry of Education Rs. 194 million.[1]

A lot has been done to expand formal training for engineers in universities and for technologists in technical schools, to provide on-the-job or in-service training in government plants. However, little has been done to promote on-the-job training for workers in the private sector. Thus workers have almost no chance to upgrade their skills and there is little upward mobility in industry. India still follows the old British pattern of apprenticeship where there is a formal legal obligation to provide training to juveniles, but where they learn by copying workmates. The situation could be greatly improved by imposing a compulsory payroll levy for this purpose, as has been done so successfully in Brazil and other countries of Latin America.[2]

The tax treatment of business is a mixture of carrot and stick. Taxes on corporate profits are much higher than under the British raj, but allowances for investment, particularly in new lines, are generous. Business incomes are subject to much higher levels of tax, but there is a good deal of evasion. The rate of industrial investment is a good deal higher than in pre-independence years.

Industrial capitalists have done reasonably well in spite of India's 'socialist' pattern, and they have not complained too loudly about it. There are three respects in which government policy towards private

[1] See Planning Commission, *Fourth Five Year Plan 1969–74*, Delhi, 1970, Chapter 17.

[2] See A. Maddison, *Foreign Skills and Technical Assistance in Economic Development*, O.E.C.D., Paris, 1965, for a description of the Brazilian system of in-service training and payroll levies.

industry may be considered to embody social objectives. These are (a) measures to help small-scale industry, (b) freedom of action for trade unions, and (c) measures to check monopoly.

Small-scale enterprises are still responsible for about 40 per cent of the net output of manufacturing and employ about three-quarters of its labour force. India has done more than most countries to promote certain forms of small-scale industry by providing subsidies and tax reliefs. Expansion in certain lines of large-scale manufacturing has also been banned to guarantee a market for small scale enterprise, financial help has been given to industrial co-operatives, and the government has sponsored industrial estates for small-scale industry. This has been partly in an effort to create as much employment as possible from industrialization, partly because the Gandhi tradition stressed the moral value of hand-loom spinning and weaving in a rural environment. The *charka* (spinning wheel) is in fact emblazoned on India's national flag. As a result of these policies, the size of the hand-loom textile industry has grown, and in 1968 represented 45 per cent of cloth output. It is estimated that 3 million hand-loom weavers were employed in that year. About 8 per cent of cloth output consisted of *khadi*, i.e. cloth which is both hand spun and hand woven. Hand spinning provided part-time employment to 1·2 million spinners. The government also sponsored labour-intensive industries like hand pounding of rice, manufacture of *gur* (a crude form of sugar), hand pressing of oil, and a small-scale manufacture of soap. In addition the government has sponsored a revival of handicrafts in metalwork and jewellery. Many of the products of these small-scale industries have been of poor quality and relatively high cost. They have been capital intensive as well as labour intensive, sometimes having a higher capital cost per unit of output than more mechanized forms of industry.[1] Furthermore, efficiency in the mill-made sector has been penalized by taxation and investment restrictions, and these have hampered exports.[2] However, a number of handicraft products which have now found an expanding domestic and export market are reasonably labour intensive.

Although there are about 4·5 million trade union members and the unions are very vigorous, there was only a negligible rise in real wages between 1948 and 1967.[3] Wages do not increase because there

[1] See the study of P. N. Dhar and A. F. Lydall, *The Role of Small Enterprise in Indian Manufacturing*, Asia Publishing House, Bombay, 1961.

[2] See M. Singh, *India's Export Trends*, Oxford, 1964.

[3] See Ministry of Finance, *Pocket Book of Economic Information 1969*, New Delhi, 1970, p. 27 shows annual industrial earnings rising by 120·5 per cent, and p. 104 shows the working-class consumer price index rising by 115·2 per cent

is a large supply of surplus labour which can be recruited easily. The major problem for industrialists is not the strength of unions, but their factionalism. Before independence there was only one trade union federation, but now there are four highly political federations, the A.I.T.U.C. (communist), I.N.T.U.C. (Congress), H.M.S. (socialist) and U.T.U.C. (halfway between communists and socialists). The disputes between them often cause stoppages to which the management is not really a party. These have been particularly severe in government steel plants. In Calcutta, labour relations are so bad and organized violence so normal that some firms are moving out of the area (e.g. Birla). These conflicts between unions have done a great deal to raise costs and have brought government frequently into industry as an arbitrator. In government plants, workers usually enjoy better working conditions and amenities than in the private sector.

It has been estimated that the twenty biggest groups controlled about 32 per cent of the share capital of the private corporate sector in 1958.[1] This share had risen from 29 per cent in 1951. Most of the leading industrial firms are old-established enterprises which pre-date independence, though there are a few which have risen since independence. Many of the big firms in India are no longer family enterprises in terms of their management personnel, and there is now a fairly large cadre of professional management. It seems clear that these big companies have been favoured by the operation of the economic control system and their relative importance is probably bigger now than in 1958. A number of measures have therefore been taken to reduce their power. In 1969, fourteen commercial banks, which controlled 70 per cent of deposits, were nationalized. These banks were controlled by the big industrial groups and favoured them in allocating credit. Life insurance companies were nationalized in 1955. A monopolies commission has been set up, and the new licensing policy laid down by the Fourth Five Year Plan is designed to restrict their activities outside the 'core' sector of industry. This is quite a departure from the earlier doctrine that the state would concentrate on the 'commanding heights' of the economy. Now the biggest firms in the private sector are being encouraged to concentrate their activities on the commanding heights.

From 1948 to 1967, total manufacturing output grew by 3·8 per cent a year, compared with 1·1 per cent from 1900 to 1946.[2] Total

[1] See R. K. Hazari, *The Structure of the Corporate Private Sector*, Asia Publishing House, Bombay, 1966, p. 40. The percentage of gross capital stock (excluding overlap) was 34·33 per cent in 1958.

[2] Figures for 1948–67 taken from official national income estimates of output in large- and small-scale manufacturing. Figures for 1900–46 from Appendix B.

industrial employment is about 20 million, of which 5 million is in factories and mines. Output per head in the organized sector is five times as great as in small-scale industry. Indian industry has expanded more slowly than that of most developing countries, but there has been a remarkable change in industrial structure towards capital goods. India is now 80 per cent self-sufficient in this sector, and is probably more autonomous in this respect than any other developing country except China, but export performance has been worse than that of almost any other country. From 1950 to 1965 only 2 per cent of the increase in industrial output went to exports, 22 per cent to import substitution and 76 per cent to meet growth in home demand.[1]

It is in the industrial sector that the government has made the biggest effort to change the structure of the Indian economy. Thus far the effort has not had much success. The output of government plants is probably only 6 per cent of the output of manufacturing as a whole, including the small-scale sector. But the capital employed in government plants is more than a third of the capital stock in manufacturing. Inefficient use of capital is due to mistakes in assessing demand, managerial inefficiency, labour difficulties and inappropriate price policy. Furthermore, these government plants have had a high import intensity.

Government policy for private industry has also tended to reduce economic growth. Overcontrol has had an adverse effect on efficiency which is publicly acknowledged, and which has now been greatly reduced. It is not possible to make a quantitative assessment of the efficiency losses to the economy as a whole from these controls, but they have obviously not been negligible.

As far as the social implications of policy are concerned, they would hardly seem to be very positive. The bigger capitalists have generally gained most from controls, inequality has increased, individual mobility has been low, real wages have been static, and consumers have been presented with a range of poor quality and high-priced goods. The main social claim for the strategy is that it has created more employment in labour-intensive, small-scale industry than would have been the case in a free market situation. It is not clear that this is so. If government had not used resources on very capital-intensive projects, they would probably have been spread more thinly elsewhere and helped generate more employment. Furthermore, it is not clear how many extra jobs were created by subsidizing small-scale

[1] See J. Ahmad, 'Import Substitution and Structural Change in Indian Manufacturing Industry 1950–1966', *The Journal of Development Studies*, April 1968. Import substitution represented 10·8 per cent of growth in consumer goods, 12·6 per cent in intermediate goods and 42 per cent in capital goods.

industry: (a) because statistics on small-scale industry are very poor; and (b) a substantial small-scale sector would have continued to exist whether the government had protected it or not. Thus the government cannot really claim credit for creating 3 million *extra* jobs in hand-loom weaving. If the government had not protected hand-loom weaving, this sector might have retained 25 per cent instead of 45 per cent of the market, i.e. it might still have provided 1·7 million jobs. Some of the 1·3 million others would have been employed in the bigger mill-made sector at higher wages, 550 million Indian consumers would have had better cloth, and export capacity would have been bigger. There may be a case for infant industry protection, but ancient industry protection is very difficult to justify.

Regional Disparities
In India it is difficult to get comparable data on levels of real income by states and even more difficult to get figures on income growth over time. Agricultural income has been rising fastest in the two wealthiest states, but there is some evidence that industrial growth has been fastest in the poorest states. The latest figures of the C.S.O. relate to 1964–5 and indicate a range from 299 rupees a head in Bihar to 575 rupees in Punjab. This is a somewhat wider regional disparity than exists in Pakistan, but it is not such an important political issue, because differences in prosperity between states are not attributable to government policy. India has a weaker central government than Pakistan and is not dominated by representatives of one region. The bitterest disputes have been about language problems rather than economics. The central government has in fact directed its investment towards some of the poorer states, and the latest formula for allocating central funds is intended to help offset income inequalities.

Table VI-3

Per Capita Income in Different Indian States 1964–5
(rupees)

Punjab	575	Mysore	420
Maharashtra	526	Kerala	393
Gujarat	523	Uttar Pradesh	374
Haryana	504	Madhya Pradesh	373
West Bengal	498	Rajasthan	356
Assam	441	Orissa	347
Andhra Pradesh	438	Jammu and Kashmir	341
Tamil Nadu	434	Bihar	299

Source: Supplied by Central Statistical Organization, Delhi.

Caste

The social problems of India are more complex than those of any other country, not merely because so many people are poor but because such a large proportion of the population consists of hereditary underprivileged groups who are regarded as inferiors by the rest of the community. These social disabilities greatly reinforce purely economic inequality and make social mobility very difficult. The main groups officially recognized as backward are the scheduled castes (outcastes) who were 14·7 per cent of the population in the 1961 census, and the scheduled tribes who were 6·8 per cent of the population.[1] In addition, one should in all honesty add the 10 per cent of the population who are Muslims, although they are not officially regarded as suffering from social discrimination. Except for the scheduled tribes, the people in these underprivileged groups are not ethnically different from other Indians, and in a modern urban environment most of them could successfully 'pass' as caste Hindus, so their segregation is not necessarily as automatic as that of Negroes in the U.S.A. In normal social intercourse, however, they would easily be identified by their names, dress, dietary and social habits, and some of the discrimination from which they suffer is worse than that suffered by Negroes in the U.S.A.

Since independence, the extreme forms of social and civic discrimination against the backward classes have been made illegal. In 1955 untouchability was made a criminal offence. Untouchables and tribals now enjoy positive discrimination in the allocation of government jobs, and both in the central and state legislatures seats have been reserved for their representatives roughly in proportion to their share of the population. They also get special educational favours, in the form of scholarships and reserved places in high schools and universities. From 1950 to 1968 the government spent Rs. 2·8 billion on special programmes for the welfare of backward classes (1 billion for scheduled castes, 1·5 billion for scheduled tribes and 0·3 billion for others).[2] The official effort to promote their welfare has therefore gone further than U.S. provisions to enhance the status of Negroes. Furthermore, their legal right to vote has never been challenged in India as has that of Negroes in the U.S.A.

These measures have certainly improved the situation of the backward classes but their position is still bad. They are greatly under-represented in the higher levels of administration. In 1968,

[1] See *Census of India 1961, Paper No. 1 of 1962, Final Population Totals*, Delhi, pp. 12–13.

[2] See *Fourth Five Year Plan 1969–74*, Planning Commission, New Delhi, 1970, p. 415.

only 2·1 per cent of the jobs in Class I of the civil service were held by untouchables as against a quota of 12 per cent. The corresponding figure for Class II was 3·1. By contrast, 18 per cent of Class IV (manual workers) are untouchables, as are almost all sweepers.[1] In the private sector, their opportunities for top jobs are even smaller. The fundamentally weak *economic* position of untouchable families makes upward movement very difficult in spite of government help in education. Post-matriculation scholarships for scheduled castes and tribes rose from 2,200 in 1951 to 145,000 in 1968, but untouchables still get less education than other groups in the population and have higher illiteracy rates. In politics, the situation is somewhat different. Adult suffrage and the reservation of seats enables the backward classes to make their numerical weight felt. Increasingly, untouchables seek to improve their status through politics and self-identification rather than through sanscritization (mimicry of upper-caste habits). The major political parties, and particularly Congress, realize that they must give a chance to untouchables in order to dissuade them from organizing a separate party of their own (like Ambedkar's party in the 1930s). There are, therefore, a reasonable number of politicians who are untouchables. However, most of them find that politics is a vehicle which can more easily be used to upgrade their own personal status rather than that of their caste.[2] There are no nation-wide parties of untouchables or tribals, as these groups have little internal homogeneity. There is no nation-wide civil rights movement such as exists amongst Negroes and liberal whites in the U.S.A., though in Bihar, the tribals have their own party, the Jharkhand party. Amongst caste Hindus the willingness to make common cause with untouchables in local disputes is probably less now than it was in the 1930s when Gandhi was leading the Congress. As younger harijans assert their rights, violence is beginning to replace the old cringing apathy, particularly at the village level.

There have, of course, been improvements in the social rights of untouchables since independence. In villages, harijans can now imitate the dress of caste Hindus. Some of them go to school and even eat school meals with caste Hindus. If they can afford it, they can now build houses in the same style as caste Hindus. But they still live in separate ghettos away from the main village, they cannot marry caste Hindus, they would not be served by barbers or washermen

[1] See Report to Parliament of N. K. Bose, Commissioner for Scheduled Castes and Tribes as quoted in *The Times*, London, April 3, 1970.
[2] A. Beteille, *Castes: Old and New*, p. 82: 'Harijan M.L.A.s and M.P.s and politically successful Harijans in general have often to move away from their caste milieu and into the social world of South Avenue or the P.C.C. office.'

who cater for caste Hindus, and they will usually be beaten or driven off if they try to use the same temples or wells as caste Hindus. The 1970 report of the Commissioner on Scheduled Castes cited a case in Guntur district of Andhra Pradesh where high-caste Hindus axed three harijans to death because they tried to draw water from the village well. They now have legal recourse against discrimination and can organize politically to protect themselves either nationally, statewise, or in village councils. However, the political system since independence has provided them with no economic favours, or more land, so their economic status is as depressed as ever. Apart from farm labouring, they are still engaged in occupations such as leather work, or sweeping, which caste Hindus regard as ritually unclean. They are still economic dependents of caste Hindus. Only a substantial redistribution of land is likely to improve their economic status.

The problems of tribal people (*adivasis*) are rather different from those of the scheduled castes (harijans). They are like the Red Indians in the U.S.A. rather than the Negroes. Although they are economically backward, they live in compact blocks in hills and forests with a separate economy and culture. They are isolated rather than segregated, ignored rather than mistreated, by the rest of the community. They are thus better off than untouchables, but it is difficult to integrate them into the rest of the economy without destroying their culture, and turning them into castes (which was the historical process by which many of them have been assimilated into the Hindu fold). Most of the money spent to help them has gone on education, and attempts to build up their local economies and protect their land against moneylenders and economic developers. As each tribal group has different languages and customs the effort to help them has met major difficulties. There have also been political difficulties with some of the tribal people who are separatists, like the Nagas.

Before 1962 the central government recognized 'other backward classes' apart from scheduled castes and tribes, but they were difficult to define, and the concept has been dropped in most states.[1] In some respects the Muslims are also a backward class whose social position is not protected by any occupational or educational favours, nor by the reserved seats they enjoyed in legislatures in the British raj. Partition greatly reduced the size of the Muslim community in India,

[1] See A. Beteille, *op. cit.*, p. 110, who estimates them to be one-seventh of the total population. The 1956 report of the Backward Classes Commission listed 2,399 groups (about three-quarters of the population) which might be regarded as backward. See M. N. Srinivas, *Caste in Modern India*, Asia Publishing House, Bombay, 1962, p. 40.

but made life more complicated for those who remained. Economically they are much better off than untouchables, but many of them now feel like aliens, and other Indians tend to regard them with suspicion. On the highest political level, two of India's presidents, Maulana Azad and Zakir Husain, have been Muslims, there is no doubt of official sincerity in wanting to avoid communal discrimination, and they still maintain Aligarh University and the Deoband Seminary as distinguished cultural centres, but Muslims occupy fewer jobs in government and the armed forces than the size of their community would warrant. None of the big corporate firms is owned by Muslims. Muslims are also backward in terms of their share of professional jobs and their level of education. 'Partition left the Muslims more demoralized than after the Mutiny. The vast majority of political leaders, army officers, administrators, doctors, engineers, lawyers and business and professional men emigrated to Pakistan, leaving behind a community leaderless and unrepresented in practically every walk of life.'[1] However, Muslims are much better off economically and socially in India than are the Hindus living in Pakistan, for the Indian government has made a serious effort to function as a secular state.

India has done a good deal more than Pakistan to improve the status of women, by increasing their educational opportunities, their role in politics, and improving their legal status. The Hindu Marriage Act of 1955 fixed sixteen years as the minimum age for marriage, and the Hindu Succession Act of 1956 gave them improved property rights. In primary education, there are now almost as many girls as boys, whereas in Pakistan the ratio is one to four. However, the only women to have seized the new opportunities are those in the upper-income groups.[2]

In cities, caste is much less obvious than it is in villages, because people are more anonymous, and many jobs in government service or modern industry have no close association with the old occupational divisions of caste. Entry to jobs is determined by contacts and education as well as by social origin. Public transport, cinemas,

---

[1] See M. R. A. Baig, 'Muslims Lack Strong Leadership', *The Times*, London, October 13, 1969.

[2] See K. Singh, *Kushwant Singh's India*, I.B.H., Bombay, 1970, pp. 69–70, 'there is no such thing as a working-class woman leader in India. At any woman's conference the accents of Oxford, Cambridge, Vassar and Smith and the chi-chi singsong of the girls schools run by European or American nuns come through distinctly. The granting of equal rights to women who are far from being the social or educational equals of men has brought a bumper harvest of important positions to the very small number of women who are capable of grasping the opportunity.'

teashops, restaurants, public education and public water supply make it difficult to observe the old standards of ritual purity or to avoid ritual pollution. However, there is a fairly close association between the economic status of the new caste-free jobs and the old ritual hierarchy of caste. The brahmins were the first to seek government jobs and tend to occupy the higher positions, just as they do in the professions. Within Indian cities different castes tend to be highly concentrated in separate residential ghettos.[1] It is also true that old ideas about status are still a hindrance to labour productivity. Nurses in urban hospitals will not usually handle bedpans or touch anything connected with excrement. B.A.s remain unemployed rather than take low status jobs, cooks will not wash dishes, bearers will not sweep floors or clean toilets, and gardeners will not sweep a garden. Senior civil servants will not carry their briefcases or files. These ritual rather than functional attitudes to work are firmly embedded throughout the economy and are an appreciable depressant on its productivity.

Education

At the time of independence, only a fifth of Indian children attended school, and one of the social goals set out in the constitution was to provide universal schooling up to the age of fourteen by 1960.

However, this target has not been reached. By 1968, according to Amartya Sen's estimates, only about 57 per cent of children aged six to eleven were attending school on a full-time basis in India as whole.[2] In some regions the figure was much lower than this. Furthermore, the enrolment ratio for girls is only about half of that for boys.

This neglect of mass education is not due to lack of funds. High school and university education has expanded much more rapidly than primary education. These higher forms of education are much more expensive than primary schooling: it costs twenty-two times as much to finance a B.A. student as a primary pupil, and eighty-nine times as much for an M.Sc. student. The main beneficiaries of higher education are the children of the higher- and middle-income groups.

[1] See Indian Anthropological Society, *Seminar on Social and Cultural Profile of Calcutta*, January 1970.
[2] See Amartya Sen, *The Crisis in Indian Education*, Shashtri Memorial Lectures, Delhi School of Economics, 1970 (mimeographed). The official statistics show a considerably higher figure (77 per cent). If we apply Sen's correction to the official figure for enrolments in the age group six to fourteen (62 per cent) it would be only 46 per cent, or less than half the group for which the constitution promised universal education by 1960.

Most higher education is free, and entrance requirements are easy, so that a substantial non-selective subsidy is given to the richest group in the population.

Professor Sen has recommended a change in higher education policy with stiffer entry requirements and higher fees, so that government spending at this level can be cut and the financial resources devoted to primary education. Apart from considerations of social justice, such a step is also justified in terms of economic returns. There is already an oversupply of university graduates, and a rupee spent on primary education is likely to have a much bigger effect on productivity than spending at the higher level. Apart from this, the quality of Indian higher educational establishments is so poor that many of them should be permanently closed.

Universal primary schooling could achieve several goals. It could help break down caste barriers by putting all village children in a common school, thus breaking down ritual barriers and ghetto segregation. School meals would help even more by breaking down dietary taboos and barriers on inter-dining, as well as raising nutritional levels. Education for all girls would help raise their social status and improve their receptivity to propaganda for birth control and better health practices.

However, most of these goals are ones to which the village oligarchs are opposed, and this is why they have not been fulfilled. The schools which do exist do not provide free education because parents have to buy school books, paper, pencils and crayons for their children. Many parents cannot afford this, so that many rural schools still use the traditional method of writing by making the letters in sand with a finger.

On the other hand, the pressure for higher education is a political imperative which it is hard to resist: 'The pressure for higher education is, of course, basically a middle-class demand, but given the nature of Indian politics today, all political parties, including those of the left, have been inclined to champion middle-class causes. The needs of the children of the poorer families, especially in the rural areas, are of course substantially sacrificed in the process.'[1]

[1] *Ibid.*

Chapter VII

The Social Impact of Pakistan's 'Functional Inequality'

In Pakistan, political power has been concentrated on the bureacratic-military elite who were the successors of the British raj. In the 1950s they functioned with a parliamentary façade of politicians and ministers drawn largely from landlord interests, but there was no genuine general election in Pakistan before 1970, and the government has been a military dictatorship since 1958. The main beneficiaries of independence have been (a) the bureaucracy and military themselves who have enjoyed lavish perquisites and have grown considerably in number, (b) the new class of industrial capitalists, (c) professional people whose numbers have grown rapidly, and (d) landlords in West Pakistan. In East Pakistan, *per capita* income has not increased since independence.

Unlike India, Pakistan has never pretended to be a welfare state. When questions of social policy have been at issue, the official doctrine has been one of 'functional inequality'. It was argued that, in the early stages of capitalist development, a high degree of inequality is necessary in order to promote savings and create entrepreneurial dynamism. The official rhetoric of this neo-calvinist doctrine is laid out in the Second Plan as follows:

'Direct taxes cannot be made more progressive without affecting the incentives to work and save. The tax system should take full account of the needs of capital formation. It will be necessary to tolerate some initial growth in income inequalities to reach high levels of saving and investment. What is undesirable is a wide disparity in consumption levels. Tax policy should, therefore, be so oriented as to direct a large part of high incomes into saving and investment rather than consumption.'

The third plan said: 'What is basic to Islamic Socialism is the creation of equal opportunities for all rather than equal distribution of wealth.' In the *Socio-Economic Objectives of the Fourth Five Year Plan (1970–75)*, November 1968, the old creed is reiterated with some doubt. There is a phrase: 'We cannot distribute poverty. Growth is vital before income distribution can improve,' but there is a lengthy reference to the conflict between economic dynamism and social justice, and a less confident note about the path that had been chosen.

It is, of course, true that Pakistan's aggregate growth was reasonably rapid in the 1960s, but there is no real evidence that inequality has contributed to the growth process. In particular, the rate of saving from private income is rather low and has actually declined since 1964.[1] Furthermore, it has become clear that the policy of 'postponing' social issues is counter-productive even if it is honestly conceived. The proponents of 'functional inequality' often claim that problems of social justice can be tackled more effectively at a 'later stage' of development when the economy is richer. However, this argument ignores the fact that the capital stock and productive capacity of the economy is geared to meeting a particular pattern of demand in particular locations, and the possibilities of usefully redistributing assets at a later stage actually diminish over time. Thus capital poured into luxury housing, large dams in West Pakistan and tractors can hardly be transferred or transformed at a later date. The production pattern affects the pattern of skills which will not be equally useful if the pattern of demand is changed at some later date. The pattern of growth chosen will also generate a particular set of vested interests in its continuance. It could be argued that the pattern of upper-class consumption and of government investment in Pakistan are still determined very largely by what the British left, i.e. colonial bungalows, cantonment areas, large dams, etc. Finally, and perhaps most important, is that 'postponing' social justice for several decades means that a whole generation of people who are dirt-poor and may well be more than half the population, are offered nothing at all by this policy. For all these reasons official faith in 'functional inequality' has waned sharply and the doctrine is under very strong attack, particularly from East Pakistan. In 1969 there were some gestures of social policy in directions already followed in India, but the basic policy mix remains similar to that under the Ayub regime, except that there is a bigger allocation for East Pakistan.

The military-bureaucratic elite which rules Pakistan is, on the whole, quite conservative. A large part of their education is Western, the organizational framework within which they work is British and their working language is English. Their houses, messes, cantonments and life-style are British colonial. Although they are at the apex of Pakistani society in terms of power, prestige and income, they persist in thinking of themselves as 'middle class'—classifying themselves subconsciously as if they were still part of British society.

[1] In 1969, gross savings were only 9·8 per cent of G.N.P.

In some ways they are a modernizing elite but their freedom of action is limited by the religious origins of the country. They feel that drastic social change on the model adopted by Ataturk in Turkey would cast doubt on the whole concept of Pakistan. Pakistan exists because the secular leaders of the Muslim community judged (correctly) that their economic welfare and political power would be much greater in an independent state than as a part of a united India. The leadership of the country has remained secular and there is no official religious hierarchy, but the orthodox *ulama* (theologians) have nevertheless been able to put a brake on certain kinds of modernization. The major manifestation of this is the backward position of women. Many women live behind veils, most of them are confined to their homes, cannot go to the movies or enter a mosque, have little access to education, are married at puberty to men chosen by their families and remain domestic drudges. Pakistan has an extremely small proportion of women in its labour force even by the standards of Muslim countries like Egypt and Turkey. Ayub Khan managed to check polygamy and give women better facilities for divorce, and reinforced his position against the orthodox by creating a progressive Islamic Research Institute,[1] but since he fell from power, religious pressure has virtually forced the government to drop propaganda for birth control. Orthodoxy is also sceptical about secular education, and Pakistan has made less progress in primary education since independence than most developing countries. More than 80 per cent of the population is illiterate—one of the highest ratios in the world. The chief modernization efforts of the bureaucratic-military elite have been to create a fairly large capitalist industrial sector in West Pakistan, and to transform the agriculture of West Pakistan into a modern capitalist economy.

In the first years of independence there was no conscious policy of industrialization. Immediately after partition, there was some stimulus to build up domestic industry because tariffs were applied to goods entering from India as well as from other countries. However, these were not high enough to affect trade patterns to a great extent and 70 per cent of trade was with India. A bigger change occurred in September 1949 when India followed the U.K. in devaluing and Pakistan did not. India refused to accept Pakistan rupees at the official rate and this led to a complete cessation of trade for eight months. When it was resumed (more or less on a barter basis), it

[1] Sir Mohammad Iqbal made it easier for Pakistan to overcome religious conservatism by emphasizing the importance of *Ijtihad*, which makes it possible to reinterpret religious doctrine in the light of modern needs; see M. Iqbal, *The Reconstruction of Religious Thought in Islam*, Luzac, London, 1960.

was limited in quantity. As a result, Pakistan's trade pattern changed drastically towards imports from other countries and there was also a greater stimulus to domestic industry to substitute for Indian goods. Finally, in 1952, Pakistan ran out of foreign reserves and tight quantitative controls were placed on imports of consumer goods from all sources.[1] From then onwards the domestic consumer goods industry had a completely protected market. Import controls have remained stringent since 1952, with only a brief relaxation in 1964, during the peak period of foreign aid. They are by far the most important reasons for the success of industrialization.

The new industrial class in Pakistan was formed largely of a small group of refugee families who had previously been traders in India, and who were able to discern the new industrial profit opportunities. The landlord class which was predominant politically in the first decade of independence had almost no role in industrial development.

The bureaucracy realized the great possibilities for industrialization and helped the new industrialists, particularly under the Ayub regime. Internal competition from foreign enterprise was restricted and they were given tax concessions. The Pakistan Industrial Credit and Investment Corporation and the Industrial Development Bank of Pakistan provided credit and access to foreign exchange. The Pakistan Industrial Development Corporation was set up in 1950 to establish public sector enterprises and was eventually responsible for about 10 per cent of industrial investment. There was no ideological commitment to public enterprise, but there were some areas in which it was felt necessary, e.g. to provide a political sop to regions which were untouched by the private sector, to build industries of strategic or political significance such as armaments or shipyards, or to compete with India. The government also wanted to help private industry by building up infrastructure investment that was too big and too long in gestation to attract private capital, e.g. electric power, natural gas and transportation, and in some fields where the 'public interest' was deemed to warrant investment, but which the private sector thought too risky or unprofitable (by its own exaggerated standards).

Because of the enormous power of government controls, and because industry was still relatively small and run by minority groups, the relationship between the bureaucracy and business has been one of patron and client. The administration had always felt superior towards business in British times, and now realized how much business was dependent on it for its markets, and its profits. Business has had to treat government as a suppliant, even though its economic,

[1] See M. A. Rahman, *Partition, Integration, Economic Growth and Interregional Trade*, Institute of Development of Economics, Karachi, 1963.

social and financial power has greatly increased. Businessmen do not push for freedom because the present system gives most of them a guaranteed income and removes the pressure of competition. If they were not under bureaucratic tutelage they would be more exposed to demands for nationalization. This relationship also satisfied the ego of bureaucrats and filled the pockets of the more corrupt amongst them. It preserved their social status because control on import of luxury goods prevented businessmen from flaunting their wealth too lavishly. In their own career they are not subject to competition but promoted by seniority and cannot be fired. Therefore the idea that businessmen should suffer bankruptcy as a penalty for inefficiency seems unjust. A large part of their own real income consists of perquisites like housing and they see nothing wrong in a business community which lives on perquisites handed out by the bureaucracy. By subjecting the business world to controls, they can fashion the whole of society in their own image. The bureaucracy therefore has a strong vested interest in controls, even though many bureaucrats realize the economic inefficiency and corruption which they breed. Under strong foreign pressure they have modified the system to bring in some element of the price mechanism, but they seem unlikely to abandon the basic idea of allocating resources by bureaucratic rationing. The situation is rather like that in the U.S.S.R. where Liberman-type reforms to increase the role of the price mechanism are resisted because they would weaken bureaucratic power. The bureaucracy claim that by helping business they have accelerated economic growth. By helping it less they might have had somewhat faster growth, a little more equity and more consumer satisfaction.

As a result of these political and social changes, the distribution of income and the sources of income have changed rapidly over the past twenty-five years. The changes have been biggest in the top layer of society. Muslims have benefited from a double displacement effect and have taken over the perquisites and power of both British and Hindus. At the same time the very thin upper crust of the colonial period has been thickened, and takes a bigger share of the national income. This does not mean that individual members of the new elite are necessarily better off than in colonial times, but there are a lot more of them.

For the mass of the people the most significant change since independence has been the increase in life expectation. In terms of living standards there have been gains in West Pakistan, but no progress in the East. Income inequality has probably increased in Pakistan since independence, and this is suggested by the pattern of growth of items of popular consumption. Foodgrain availability per head rose from 14·9 ounces a day in 1949 to 15·3 ounces in 1968.[1] This is a smaller increase than in India, where consumption rose from 13·9 ounces a day in 1951 to 15·4 ounces in 1969.[2] However, in the early 1950s, West Pakistan had lost its normal export market in India, and consumption was higher than normal because of the trade-boycott. Cotton cloth consumption *per capita* increased by 36 per cent from 1950 to 1968, which is a bigger increase than in India.

Table VII-1

Percentage Distribution of Pre-Tax Income in Pakistan in 1963

Percentage of households	Urban	Rural	Total
0–10	2·2	2·5	2·5
10–20	3·8	4·0	4·0
20–30	4·5	5·5	5·0
30–40	5·0	6·5	6·0
40–50	5·5	7·5	7·0
50–60	7·0	8·0	8·5
60–70	9·0	10·5	9·5
70–80	11·0	13·0	12·5
80–90	15·0	15·0	15·0
90–100	37·0	27·5	30·0

Source: A. Bergan, 'Personal Income Distribution and Personal Savings in Pakistan; 1963–4', *The Pakistan Development Review*, Summer 1967, pp. 202–4.

Statistical estimates of income distribution are still very shaky. The Central Statistical Office of the government has published figures for 1966–7 which show the top 20 per cent of the population with 31 per cent of household income in East Pakistan and about 34 per cent in West Pakistan. It is fairly obvious that these figures understate the income of the higher groups, for there are few countries with this degree of equality. A more careful study for the year 1963–4 shows the top 20 per cent with 45 per cent of the income (see Table VII-1). This was a bumper crop year in East Pakistan, when the poorest part of the population had a better share than normal, so it also understates inequality, but the estimate is the best we have. It

[1] See Planning Commission, *Outline of the Fourth Five Year Plan (1970–5)*, Islamabad, 1970, p. 5.

[2] See Ministry of Finance, *Economic Survey 1969–70*, Delhi, 1970, p. 72.

suggests that income inequality is smaller in Pakistan than in India (see Table VI-1). Although the comparability of tables VI-1 and VII-1 is limited by the poor quality of the statistics, it is feasible that income distribution may be more equal in Pakistan than in India. In West Pakistan there was a far lower proportion of landless labourers than in India at the time of independence, and although the porportion has risen in West Pakistan, it is still very much lower than in India. In East Pakistan, the proportion of landless labourers was distinctly lower than in India at independence,[1] and East Pakistan's land reform was more far-reaching than in India, because most zamindars and many of the tenants-in-chief were Hindus who fled the country. In both East and West Pakistan money-lenders were usually Hindus and fled at the time of partition. Another factor which affects the situation is that Pakistan has a smaller urban population ratio than India, and in both countries income is more unequal in the cities than in the countryside.

In Pakistan, income tax is considerably lower than in India, and direct taxes are only 2 per cent of national product.[2] Total public sector spending on social services such as health, education, housing, water and sewerage is only about 3 per cent of national product, and most of the benefits of this go to the upper income groups. In education only a third of expenditure goes to the primary level, in health most expenditure is for urban areas; nearly all public housing projects and housing subsidies are for middle and upper income groups, nearly all spending on amenities is for urban areas. In past plans, schemes for unversity development have usually been fulfilled, but primary schools building was well below target, programmes to build medical schools were fulfilled and rural health centres neglected, targets for civil service housing overfulfilled and rural sanitation neglected. The third plan allocated less than half a rupee per head for water and sanitation in rural areas over a five-year period, whereas the urban population got Rs. 13·5 each plus municipal spending.[3]

[1] See S. J. Patel, *Agricultural Labourers in Modern India and Pakistan*, Current Book House, Bombay, 1952, p. 31.

[2] Out of a labour force of 42 million, only 300,000 pay income tax. Liability to tax starts at twenty times the average *per capita* income, and the farming population are completely exempt. Rates do not rise as steeply as in India, and there are bigger exemptions for saving. A man with an annual income of Rs. 50,000 will pay only Rs. 4,670 in tax if he makes the qualifying investments; in India he would pay Rs. 17,000. Corporate taxation rates are about the same as in India, but with more tax privileges. Land tax is not progressive and is a minor burden.

[3] See A. Maddison, 'Social Development of Pakistan 1947–70', Economic

We shall now analyse the impact of economic development on the following groups: (1) bureaucrats; (2) the armed forces; (3) other professions; (4) agriculture; (5) industry, and then look at the problem of regional inequality.

1. *Bureaucrats*

The power of the bureaucracy has increased since independence. It is not checked by a parliament or a free press, official reports are suppressed when found embarrassing, and the growth of a dirigiste control system and a large public sector have strengthened the possibilities of patronage and corruption. The size of the bureaucracy has grown considerably since independence, and the biggest expansion has been at the top. At independence there were only about 200 Muslims who were Class I civil servants in India,[1] now there are 3,000 in Pakistan. The linchpin is the Civil Service of Pakistan (C.S.P.), an elite group of 500 generalists who are the successors to the I.C.S. and hold most of the key jobs. There are about 2,500 other Class I officers in the central and provincial government and administrative agencies. Underneath there are three other classes of government employees numbering about 500,000 in all. There are about 6,000 officers in Class II where the minimum qualification is a B.A. degree. Class III consists of about 100,000 clerks, typists and stenographers (all males) who have had a secondary education, can read and write English (but seldom understand it properly when spoken). They do routine work, type and keep the files and ledgers in good order. Class IV consists largely of manual workers, peons and sweepers. Peons are flunkeys who carry files, messages and tea, and salute their superiors. Most of them have completed primary education, but do not know English. Less than one per cent of the civil service is in Class I, whereas Class IV is huge and, for the most part, functionally redundant. Very little in-service training is provided to Class III or Class IV personnel and they have no hope of rising from one class to another.

Bureaucratic power is heavily concentrated on the C.S.P. Entry to this service is by examination at the age of twenty-one or twenty-two.

Report, Centre for International Affairs, Harvard University, 1971.

[1] At the time of partition, there were 1,157 officers in the Indian Civil Service and Indian Political Service of whom 101 were Muslims. Ninety-five of these opted for Pakistan. Only two of them were from East Pakistan. See Khalid bin Sayeed, *The Political System of Pakistan*, Oxford University Press, Karachi, 1967, p. 132. In addition, there were Muslims in the police and technical services. Since independence there has been a very big increase in the proportion of Bengalis in the higher civil service.

In their first years (after initial training which took place in England until 1959), they serve as sub-divisional officers. Later in their careers, after a spell of secretariat work, they will come back to field work as deputy commissioners or commissioners for a district. The average district now has close to 2 million people. The district officer is the chief magistrate, controlling the police and revenue collection, and is responsible for all economic development work. The local heads of all government agencies are his subordinates. Under Ayub, there was a system of elected local government, but the district officer effectively dominates any local government authority, whether rural or municipal. The C.S.P. also occupy most of the politically strategic positions in central and provincial ministries, though there are now a good many non-C.S.P. personnel in senior positions who do more specialized work, particularly in the Planning Commission or in the twenty government corporations.

Civil servants are not well paid. In real terms, Class I officers are worse off than their British counterparts who had similar salaries thirty years ago when prices were much lower. However, Pakistan income tax hardly affects civil servants, even at the top level (this is not surprising in a regime dominated by bureaucrats), and most of them have substantial tax-free perquisites. Many get lavish official housing at 7·5 per cent of their salary (compared with 15 per cent in India) which involves a substantial subsidy,[1] some household amenities are subsidized, medical expenses are reimbursed and they get free travel home on leave. At the top level there are official cars, guest houses, etc. Office flunkeys will often work as servants in their houses. Civil servants also have job security, promotion by seniority and retirement on pension at age fifty-five. These perquisites have become more important as the real value of salaries has dropped. Perquisites are important not only as income, but as badges of rank. They highlight the professional immobility between classes and homogenize consumption patterns within each class. A Class I officer's 'residence' (it is never called a house or a home) will be quite different from that of a Class II officer. There are no shadings of ambiguity to mitigate the segregation.

[1] Two-thirds of the public housing built during the Third Plan (1965–70) was for civil servants. In addition to public housing the government provided local authorities with loans for developing housing plots (Rs. 257 million during the Third Plan). Most of these were for upper-class housing in areas developed by improvement trusts and housing corporations like Gulberg in Lahore, Gulshan in Dacca, and Satellite Town in Rawalpindi. The developed plots were sold on a non-profit basis, i.e. well below their market value to civil servants, military and other officially favoured clients, whereas they should obviously have been sold by auction. There have been no effective limits on the size of plots.

Since independence, the licensing system has brought bureaucrats and business into very close contact: in many cases, the civil servant who hands over a licence is giving away something of very great value to the recipient, and it is only natural that he will be tempted to take a cut, or that he will be offered one by competitors for his favours. As a result there has been large-scale corruption, and 303 Class I civil servants were suspended under Martial Law Regulation 58 in December 1969 for suspected dishonesty or misuse of powers.

At any stage of time it is possible to remove corruption by exemplary punishment, or increases in basic pay, but unless the bureaucratic-business relation is changed, the problem will persist.

Some of the problems of the bureaucracy were analysed in the report of the Cornelius Commission set up by President Ayub.[1] This report was suppressed for seven years because it was too critical of the C.S.P. The Commission recommended an integration of all the services and a simplification of grades, the provision of better career incentives and sanctions, and better training. Its most controversial proposal was the abolition of the C.S.P.—an end to the system in which district administration was dominated by one man, and a greater role for functional specialists in running ministries. Unfortunately, the Cornelius report did not deal with the relations between the bureaucracy and the economy, nor did it recommend any substantial change in the system of payment by perquisites (the consequences of which were perhaps not as obvious in 1962 as they are now).

2. *Armed Forces*

Like the bureaucracy, the armed forces are a heritage of the British raj and have grown considerably since independence. Before the Second World War the Indian armed forces numbered less than 200,000. The officer corps was almost entirely British and there were only a handful of Hindu and Muslim officers. During the war there was a big expansion, and demobilization was slowed down after the war in anticipation of partition. Pakistan therefore inherited armed forces of about 120,000 men and a Muslim officer corps of about 1,000.[2] However, only 100 of the officers held the rank of captain and above.[3] Now there are about 300,000 military personnel. In the

---

[1] See *Report of the Pay and Services Commission 1959–1962*, Government of Pakistan, 1969.

[2] See A. L. Venkateswaran, *Defence Organization in India*, Ministry of Information and Broadcasting, Delhi, 1967, for a description of the situation at partition.

[3] See Khalid bin Sayeed, *op. cit.*

colonial period, the area of West Pakistan was the major recruiting ground for the Indian army, and its inhabitants were considered 'martial races'. Bengalis were not recruited after the 1857 Mutiny in which they had taken a leading part. Since independence the situation has changed a little but the traditional predominance of West Pakistanis in the army still persists. Less than 5 per cent of army officers are from East Pakistan which contains 55 per cent of the country's population.

As in colonial times, both soldiers and officers serve on a career basis and there has been no attempt to use the army for development purposes or popular education as in Iran, Israel or China. The Sandhurst tradition is dominant. Islam is not stressed. The social life of officers is still modelled on the pre-war British pattern. There are still polo-playing subalterns, blimpish generals, Scottish bands and plenty of spit and polish. Promotion from the ranks to the officer corps is rare, though entry to the officer corps by people of humble origin has been eased by the creation of cadet colleges and removal of fees for officer training.

The gap between the pay of privates and officers is smaller than in colonial times. The salaries of officers compare with those of Class I civil servants, and are lower in real terms than those of pre-war officers in the Indian army. However, the amenities and perquisites of army life are substantial. The armed forces have special commissaries where they can buy supplies cheaply, new houses for officers are often luxury dwellings and the military have their own schools, sewerage, hospitals and dairies which are generally of higher standard than those available for civilians.[1] Furthermore, most of the military live in special 'cantonments' which were created by the British as select residential areas. They have better roads, street lighting, sanitation, health and educational facilities than other urban areas and are subsidized by the military budget. Many of the most prosperous civilian population also live in the cantonment areas because amenities are better and taxes are lower there. The cantonments are located on prime land in many cities, which seems a distinct anachronism in an independent country. The armed forces are probably the most efficient body in the country, and in spite of a military regime they are not overstaffed with senior officers. It seems a pity that some more of the talents of the armed forces cannot be used for development work, e.g. helping with public works or running a system of national service to help mobilize and train human resources. The only case in which military talents were applied

[1] See M. Ayub Khan, *Friends Not Masters*, Oxford University Press, Lahore, 1967, p. 43.

to civilian purposes was in building up Pakistan International Airlines, which has been outstandingly successful.

3. Other Professional Groups

In terms of growth in numbers, the new Muslim professional class has done well in Pakistan, displacing both Hindus and British, and in addition taking a bigger share of national income. Relative to the military and bureaucracy, they gained more from the flight of Hindus.

The biggest group are teachers, of whom there are about 350,000, and their number has trebled since independence. However, their social status is extremely low and primary teachers are usually paid less than unskilled workers, so they can hardly be considered prime beneficiaries of economic growth.

The next biggest group consists of lawyers, who enjoy relatively large incomes. Their number has not increased as fast as other professional groups but, before independence, a large proportion of lawyers were Hindus, particularly in East Pakistan.

There are about 16,000 doctors practising in Pakistan as compared with about 6,000 Muslim doctors at independence. The profession works largely for the urban population and is relatively prosperous, but lucrative job openings for doctors are limited and half the new doctors emigrate.[1]

The number of professional people in business is not known, but it must have increased enormously since there was little industry in pre-independence days, and all banking and insurance were conducted by British and Hindus.

There are undoubtedly more journalists in Pakistan now than there were in pre-independence days, but their professional opportunities are, of course, severely restricted by censorship. Opportunities for politicians have been even more limited under the military regimes since 1958.

Other groups like artists or sportsmen have had few opportunities to develop their professions as the government has done very little to promote cultural or sporting activities.

4. Agriculture

There are about 30 million people occupied in agriculture out of a labour force of 42 million; in East Pakistan there are nearly 21 million (84 per cent of the labour force), in the West a little over 9 million (53 per cent of the labour force). Agricultural output stagnated in the 1950s, partly because of the loss of markets in other parts of the

[1] See R. A. Karwanski, 'Doctors and Medical Personnel in Pakistan 1960–1985', Planning Commission, Islamabad, 1968 (mimeographed).

subcontinent for rice, wheat and jute, partly because of the government policy of price controls, and export levies on farm products. In the 1960s, price policy has been different, with subsidies for fertilizer and diffusion of new seeds which raised productivity. However, most of the benefits of this have been concentrated in West Pakistan. In Pakistan as a whole, total crop output rose by 2·3 per cent a year from 1947 to 1966, in East Pakistan by 1·6 and in West Pakistan by 3·2 per cent. The total agricultural labour force rose by 1·9 per cent a year, by 2·3 per cent in East Pakistan and 1·0 per cent a year in West Pakistan.[1] This means that production per employee rose by 2·2 per cent a year in the West, and fell by 0·7 per cent a year in the East.

The disparity in agricultural growth between East and West Pakistan was probably even greater in the fifty years preceding independence than it has been since 1947. According to Blyn, crop output grew by 1·6 per cent a year in Greater Punjab in the half century preceding independence. In Sind, production grew faster than in Punjab, as the area was a desert in the 1890s and had 5 million acres of irrigated land at independence. It would not therefore be surprising if the agricultural output of the area which is now West Pakistan, did not increase by as much as 2 per cent a year from the 1890s to independence. By contrast, in the area which is now East Pakistan, output was stagnant in the half century preceding independence.[2]

One reason for the growth differential in the colonial period, as now, is that there was large investment in irrigation in the West and virtually none in the East. The British government irrigated 18 million acres of West Pakistan by government canals (*a*) because it was profitable, and (*b*) because it recruited more than half of the Indian army from the Muslims and Sikhs who lived there and who had been loyal in the 1857 Mutiny. Apart from the government investment, agriculture benefited from the fact that many of the people in it were new settlers, and a fair proportion of them had seen service in the Indian army which gave them a degree of sophistication and technical training as well as money in the form of pensions. There was therefore more dynamism and more private investment in the West Pakistan area than the average for India, more money-

---

[1] The labour force figures are rough estimates. For 1951–61 we used the figures on male workers from the census (the definition of female employment changed) and linked these to 1961–70 from K. Ruud 'Some Tentative Manpower and Employment Estimates (Targets) for the Fourth Plan', Planning Commission, Islamabad, September 1969 (mimeographed).

[2] See G. Blyn, *op. cit.*, pp. 119 and 222.

lending and a greater concentration on commercial crops. There were also fewer untouchables and landless labourers, and caste was less important amongst Muslims, Sikhs and the tribal population than it was in India as a whole. The 'built-in depressants' were hardly present in this area. East Bengal, by contrast, was the area whose relative economic status suffered most by British rule. In the seventeenth century, Bengal was generally considered by travellers such as Bernier to be the most prosperous part of India, but at independence it was probably one of the poorest. The decline was biggest in industry, but may also have affected agriculture.

From 1947 to 1965, the cropped area in West Pakistan grew by 1·7 per cent a year which is faster than the 1 per cent a year expansion in Greater Punjab from 1891 to 1941. The supply of irrigation water grew by 78 per cent from 1947 to 1970, or about 2·5 per cent a year.[1] By 1970, 31 million acres were irrigated out of 40 million cultivated. In the last half century of British rule the irrigated area also rose by about 2·5 per cent a year (about fourfold from 1891 to 1947). However, the quality of irrigation has improved in the post-war period because canal irrigation has been supplemented by tubewell irrigation which not only provides a more reliable source of water but reduces salinity by lowering the water table, whereas canal irrigation has caused waterlogging and salinity, because of inadequate drainage. By 1969 there were 78,000 private tubewells in West Pakistan.

There has also been a rapid increase in the use of fertilizer and insecticide (with the help of government subsidies) and new seeds (Mexipak wheat and Irri-rice), which have proved ideal in West Pakistan conditions with its vast supply of solar energy and reliable irrigation.

During the 1950s, West Pakistani agriculture was depressed because of the collapse of its export market in India, but the rapid growth of population has more than restored the old demand for foodgrains, and industrial demand for cotton within Pakistan has greatly increased. As a result, output increased much faster in the 1960s than in the 1950s.

Although there were few landless labourers in West Pakistan

[1] The public irrigation supply of surface water rose from 45·6 million acre feet (at the water course) to 63 million acre feet, and 6,700 large public tubewells yielded 7 million acre feet of ground water in 1970 compared with virtually zero in 1947. In the private sector, 78,000 tubewells produced 14 million acre feet in 1970 (none in 1947), and 200,000 Persian wheels produced 3·6 million acre feet (same as 1947). These data are taken from the *Fourth Plan Outline*, and from P. Lieftinck, A. R. Sadove and T. C. Creyke, *Water and Power Resources of West Pakistan*, Vol. I, I.B.R.D., Johns Hopkins, Baltimore, 1968.

before independence, there were plenty of big landlords. The Punjab and Sind were incorporated in the British raj only in 1849, and as the British wanted local support in an area close to the frontier, they interfered less with feudal privileges there than they did elsewhere in British India. Landlords exercised political and spiritual dominance over their submissive and ignorant tenants. Independence did little to reduce their economic and political status, and they were a very influential political group from 1947 to 1958. Ayub Khan had this to say about their attitude to land reform:

'The main purpose of the so-called reforms introduced in West Pakistan before the Revolution was to preserve the privileges of the *zamindars* and not to secure the rights of the tenants. The landlords subverted all attempts at a more rational distribution of land through the influence they exercised over the political parties. Even the very mild reforms enacted in the Punjab in 1952 were annulled by Malik Firoz Khan Noon, the Republican Chief Minister, in 1953. Apart from its social and economic consequences, such concentration of power naturally hampered the free exercise of political institutions. Democracy could never have a chance so long as the big landlords enjoyed protected constituencies immune to any pressure of public opinion.'[1]

Ayub also describes the ownership situation as follows: '50 per cent of the available land in the Punjab, a little less than 50 per cent in the North-West Frontier, and over 80 per cent in the Sind was in the possession of a few thousand absentee landowners.' After Ayub took power there was a land reform in West Pakistan in 1959 which established ceilings on landownership, and broke up some of the bigger holdings (with compensation). About 2·3 million acres were surrendered by 6,000 landlords. In addition, 0·7 million acres of *jagir* land were surrendered. This measure hardly amounted to a social revolution. The ceiling for irrigated land was 500 acres, and for unirrigated land, 1,000 acres (as compared with 50 acres or less in India). The land surrendered was only 6 per cent of the total cultivated area, in general it was the worst land, and to some extent the provisions of the law were evaded by splitting up large holdings among family members. The recipients of land were usually those who happened to be tenants of larger landlords. Some peasants with weak tenancy rights were dispossessed by landlords asserting a claim to be direct cultivators of as much of their land as possible, and the proportion of landless agricultural labourers increased substantially

[1] See M. Ayub Khan, *op. cit.*, p. 87.

Table VII-2

Size Distribution of Operational Holdings in
Pakistani Agriculture in 1960

EAST PAKISTAN

Size range of family holding (acres)	Percentage of rural households	Percentage of area
no land	26·0	0·0
under 1	18·0	3·2
1–2·5	20·2	13·0
2·5–5	19·5	26·4
5–25	16·0	52·6
25 and above	0·3	4·8

WEST PAKISTAN

no land	11·3	0·0
under 1	13·5	0·7
1–2·5	15·6	2·8
2·5–5	14·7	5·9
5–25	37·8	47·9
25 and above	7·1	42·7

Source:
Figures on size distribution of holdings from *1960 Pakistan Census of Agriculture*, Karachi, 1962–3. Figures on the proportion of landless labourers to the agricultural labour force excluding family workers from *Census of Pakistan, Population*, Vol. I, Karachi, 1961, Table V-27. This was taken as a rough approximation to the proportion of landless households. It should be noted that the figures refer to operational holdings and not to ownership (for which I was not able to find a distributive table). Ownership will be more unequal than is shown here because the holding is attributed to the operator in this table, whether he be owner, tenant or sharecropper. In West Pakistan 39 per cent of holdings were held by tenants, 22·5 per cent by owner-cum-tenants, and the rest by proprietors. In East Pakistan 1·1 per cent was cultivated by tenants, 45·2 per cent by owner-cum-tenants and the rest by proprietors.

from 1951 to 1961.[1] Table VII-2 throws some light on the distribution of land (although it refers to operational holdings rather than ownership). Fifty-five per cent of the rural population have less than 8·5 per cent of the land to cultivate.

The main benefits of the expansion in agricultural output in West Pakistan in the 1960s have gone to the large capitalist farmers and

[1] See *Census of Pakistan, Population*, Vol. I, Karachi, 1961, Table V-27.

the bigger peasant holdings. 'Over one-third of the cultivable area in West Pakistan is in holdings of less than 12½ acres each. . . . These small farms generally do not possess the means to purchase better seeds, more fertilizer, adequate water and other elements of the new agricultural technology. They also need more extension services, readily available credit and better marketing facilities.'[1] In fact, 77 per cent of the farms in West Pakistan are smaller than 12·5 acres, so the implication of this statement by the Planning Commission is that only a quarter of the farmers have reaped substantial benefit from the 'green revolution'.

Large landowners in West Pakistan have had a very large increase in income in the 1960s but they pay less than 2 per cent of their income in tax. Agriculture is exempt from income tax, and land tax is a negligible and non-progressive burden. In addition, the canal water which they buy from the government is heavily subsidized. With the new technology, farming has become extremely profitable, and many big farmers are setting up mechanized farms using tractors which they buy cheaply thanks to a low tariff and favourable exchange rate.

In East Pakistan, the agricultural situation was completely different both before and after independence. The dominant class in rural areas were zamindars. Most of these were Hindus and for this reason zamindari reform was implemented quickly and took away the land which zamindars did not themselves cultivate. As in India, the main beneficiaries were the bigger tenants of zamindars. Apart from the exodus of zamindars there was also an outflow of Hindu money-lenders who found it difficult to collect outstanding debts. Small peasants who had been tenants of tenants and the landless labourers gained almost nothing from the reforms. There are many more completely landless labourers in East than in West Pakistan (2·5 million in 1961 as compared with 0·6 million in the West). Similarly the peasants who do have farms are poorer than in the West. The average farm size in East Pakistan is 3·5 acres, compared with 10 acres in the West. The Eastern farm has an average crop intensity of 1·4, whereas for the Western farm it is 0·9, but it is clear neverthe-less that average farm income per head is substantially lower in the East. It is also more unstable because of the high incidence of flooding, and the trend of output has grown much more slowly than in the West. In fact, *per capita* farm output is substantially lower than it was at independence.

The main change affecting production since independence has been the increase in the cropped area by 0·9 per cent a year, considerably

[1] *The Socio-Economic Objectives of the Fourth Five Year Plan (1970–1975)*, Planning Commission, Islamabad, 1968.

less than in West Pakistan. Some help has been given to farmers for small-scale irrigation with low lift pumps and tubewells, but the increase in irrigated area has only been 1·3 million acres since independence. It is difficult to undertake really large-scale irrigation and flood control because (a) the problem is so massive and a great deal of preparatory investigative work is still necessary, (b) effective work would depend on Indian co-operation and willingness to invest very large amounts of money, because both the Ganges and Brahmaputra flow through Indian territory before reaching Pakistan. The effort to develop new varieties of seed to improve rice yields has been slower to produce effective results than similar work on wheat and rice for West Pakistan. Finally, the problem of providing landless labourers with land through further land reform is difficult in a country where there are no large landowners, although 57 per cent of the land is in holdings above 5 acres.

The Pakistan government is now committed to making a much heavier investment effort in East Pakistan, but it remains to be seen what effective scope there is for large-scale irrigation.

One programme which acted as a mild palliative to the East Pakistan rural situation was the Works Programme. The Works Programme was introduced in 1962 after several years of experience with Village AID which was an ineffective programme of rural uplift with a rather small infusion of funds. Village AID was a multi-purpose programme encompassing agricultural extension, cottage industry, health and social activity as well as rural works. The scheme was administered largely by government officials, and village participation in public works was expected to be on a voluntary basis. The Works Programme was considerably larger than Village AID (Rs. 640 million were spent in the Second Plan compared with Rs. 100 million on Village AID in the first). It concentrated primarily on creating employment in public works, and the participants were paid 2 rupees a day (which was a slightly higher rate than for some kinds of unskilled labour). The administration was entrusted to the organs of local government (the basic democracies created by President Ayub), which acquired control over funds and decided what work to undertake. Three-quarters of the funds in East Pakistan were spent on roads, and the rest went mainly on drainage and flood control.

There is a good deal of argument about the efficacy of the programme. J. W. Thomas has suggested[1] that the work accomplished

---

[1] See J. W. Thomas, *Rural Public Works and East Pakistan's Development*, Harvard Advisory Group, September 1968.

was of very substantial benefit to the economy and had a high benefit-cost ratio of 4 : 1. Rehman Sobhan has criticized the programme because of misappropriation of funds and because he feels that greater emphasis should have been given to drainage, irrigation and flood control, rather than low-quality roads which will not last long and cannot be used by heavy vehicles.[1]

In fact, it would not be surprising if the Works Programme had been inefficient in terms of work accomplished. It was a fairly large-scale effort, launched with little preparation, involving delegation of power to local bodies with no previous works experience, and with no carefully prepared projects. Its primary objective was to provide new hopes and aspirations in the village and to test the capacity of local bodies to devise schemes of their own.

The real criticism of the programme is not that it made some mistakes, but that it is still small in relation to the size of the surplus labour problem. In 1969 the works programme created 390,000 man years of employment in East Pakistan.

A larger programme would be feasible if labour could be mobilized without payment. It is doubtful whether any country has ever been able to mobilize a truly voluntary effort of public works on a large scale except in time of national emergency. However, compulsory service is often accepted fairly cheerfully if it is imposed by a government which is popular, or which is bringing about major social change, and if the burden of service is felt to be universally and fairly shared. It has been suggested that peasants provide labour service in lieu of land tax, but this might well be considered a feudal imposition, and one would not know in advance how much labour would be offered. Probably the most efficient form of compulsory labour would be a period of national service for young people to be performed in the dry months of the year when they were not needed on the farms. It would be necessary to feed these conscript workers as they would be away from home for part of the period, and they might well lack the stamina for work without free food. Here again, it would obviously be difficult to mobilize more than a fraction of the 'unemployed' without running into substantial organizational costs.

Another problem with a really large-scale works programme is to find suitable projects. Roads are probably the most straightforward, because the right of way is normally established and construction problems are fairly similar everywhere. Irrigation and drainage are

---

[1] See R. Sobhan, *Basic Democracies, Works Programme and Rural Development in East Pakistan*, University of Dacca, no date.

more complicated because they involve private land rights to a greater extent, and hydrological knowledge. Buildings require even more supervisory skill.

It is clear, therefore, that the works programme approach will not solve the problem of 'unemployment'. It can simply mitigate it. But it would be useful if its work-spreading philosophy could be infused into other programmes.

5. *Industry*

At the time of independence there was almost no modern industry in Pakistan. Economic activity was concentrated almost entirely on agriculture which provided other parts of India with food and raw materials. The jute of East Bengal was manufactured in Calcutta, and West Pakistan's cotton was used by the manufacturing industry of Ahmedabad and Bombay.

Since independence, Pakistani industry has taken a great leap forward, and a large new class of Muslim businessmen has emerged. The growth of capitalist enterprise has been deliberately fostered by government, which has been the universal patron of businessmen.

Nevertheless, the degree of control over the private sector in allocating scarce materials, fixing prices, issuing capital, and allocating imports was just as high in Pakistan as in India until 1959.

There has been no explicit philosophy of public ownership in Pakistan, and P.I.D.C. has generally (but not always) started up government enterprises only in pioneering lines which private enterprise was unwilling or unable to develop. The government has not tried to maintain certain sectors of activity as a government monopoly. Official ideology has favoured private enterprise, and some government enterprises have been sold off to the private sector. However, the government sector in Pakistan produces about the same proportion of industrial output as in India. The profit record of public corporations is somewhat better than in India, and their management is more independent and better paid.

The main ways in which government has helped have been as follows:

(*a*) There have been severe restrictions since 1949 on all trade and service transactions with India (amounting to a complete boycott since 1965) which was the main supplier of industrial goods in pre-war years to the area which became Pakistan. Substantial tariff protection and quotas have kept out goods from other countries, particularly consumer goods whose import was largely

banned. This created a captive market for new Pakistani entrepreneurs, who were thus presented with unrivalled profit opportunities. Furthermore, foreign business activity and foreign private
enterprise in Pakistan was restricted;

(b) The government supplied industry with *cheap machinery*. The
exchange rate was overvalued and consumer goods imports were
either banned or subject to very high tariffs, but capital goods
entered duty free or at low tariffs, and they could usually be paid
for at the official exchange rate, whereas other goods were more
expensive because of the bonus voucher system which operated as a
multiple exchange rate;

(c) Government also provided industry with *cheap raw materials*.
Jute and cotton were at first subjected to large export taxes which
kept their domestic price below international levels. Later these were
removed, but jute and cotton exports do not attract bonus vouchers
and hence are less favoured than exports of manufactured jute and
cotton goods;

(d) Until 1969, the government helped supply industry with *cheap
labour* by suppressing trade union activity.[1] This kept real wages

[1] See *Labour Policy of Government of Pakistan*, Ministry of Health, Labour and
Family Planning, July 1969, p. 1: 'In Pakistan, the growth of Trade Unions has
been extremely slow. It is estimated by Trade Union leaders themselves that their
total membership does not exceed 5 to 10 per cent of the entire industrial and
commercial labour force. There have been three main reasons for this. Firstly,
it has been the ignorance of the workers themselves who have too readily adopted
the model of a tenant-landlord relationship in industrial life. It is only recently
that the workers have begun to realize that this sort of feudal relationship is not
necessarily in their interest. The second reason for the slow growth of Trade
Unions has been the attitude of the employers, who, being by and large first
generation industrialists, have failed to realize the contribution which a contented
and well-motivated worker can make to productivity and profitability. They have
looked upon Trade Unions as instruments for extortion rather than as institutions
through which mutual give and take can lead to a peaceful resolution of conflict
and possibly higher productivity. They have therefore used all sorts of unfair
means such as the creation of "pocket" unions, victimization of the office
bearers of genuine Trade Unions, etc., to inhibit the growth of Trade Unions.
And finally, the third reason for the slow growth of Trade Unions has been the
attitude of the Government itself which, too conscious of the need to keep
production going regardless of the human and social costs involved, has discouraged, and in many cases prohibited, the expression of industrial conflict
rather than trying to resolve it. It is obvious that, just as in national life the
Government failed to appreciate the importance of political processes, so also in
industrial relations, it had not realized that conflicts cannot be resolved by their
suppression; they can only be resolved through a process of mutual give and
take, which is only possible through strong Trade Union institutions, particularly
in labour surplus economies where, otherwise the individual worker is in a weak
bargaining position in relation to the employer.'

constant or declining until the strikes at the end of the Ayub regime in 1969;[1]

(e) The government has given business *cheap capital* in the form of low interest loans from the Industrial Development Bank of Pakistan, P.I.C.I.C. and other agencies. They have also had very substantial tax concessions and tax holidays, and business was permitted to carry out substantial tax evasion without much attempt at penalization.

Although the bureaucracy has done so much to foster business interests, it should not be forgotten that business taxation is *relatively* high. In theory corporate tax is about half of corporate income, and although the burden is lightened considerably by exemptions and evasion, it is still true that the tax burden is bigger on business than it is on other high income groups. It may well be about 20 per cent of the true profit income of business, whereas large landlords pay less than 2 per cent of their income in direct taxes.

The government has done little to promote technical training in industry but, until now, development has taken place in fields which were technically rather simple, i.e. cotton and jute textiles, in which a high degree of skill was not required. Wherever technical skills were required there has been a tendency to import them from abroad, but now that industry is becoming more technically complex there are likely to be more significant managerial and technocratic problems of the type that have plagued the more complex industries in India.

Production in the modern industrial sector increased by 15 per cent a year from 1950 to 1966. Mill-made cotton cloth expanded from 86 million yards in 1947 to 739 million in 1966. Jute goods rose from virtually zero to 404 thousand tons in 1966, cigarettes from 320 million in 1949 to 32 billion in 1966, sugar from 35 thousand tons in 1947 to 417 thousand in 1966. Tea was the only real manufacturing industry which had existed at partition, and it grew much more slowly from 49 thousand tons in 1947 to 67 thousand in 1966.

From 1949 to 1968 the output of small-scale industry increased 60 per cent, whereas output of large-scale industry increased twelve-fold. Small-scale industry has received some tax concessions and technical help from government, but official patronage for industry has been concentrated on large-scale firms, which do not have the

---

[1] See A. R. Khan, 'What has been happening to Real Wages in Pakistan?', *Pakistan Development Review*, Autumn 1967, and A. R. Khan 'Exercises in Minimum Wages and Wage Policy', P.I.D.E., Karachi, May 1969 (mimeographed).

same network of sub-contracting relations with small industry which was so successful in exploiting labour-intensive technologies in Japan. Government has given little help in design, marketing and training for handicrafts, so that Pakistan handicraft products are generally of poor quality, and are only a pale shadow of the glories of Moghul craftsmen (who were mostly Muslims).

At independence, there were only two important industrial families in Pakistan, Ispahani and Adamjee, who were in the tea business. Both of these have expanded their interests and new family groups have also entered industry. The new opportunities were seized by very few families,[1] and industrial, financial and commercial power have become very highly concentrated. Up to 1964, over two-thirds of assets sold by government to industry were bought by the leading families.[2] Detailed analysis of this concentration is hard to find, but the Chief Economist of the Planning Commission suggested that 'the top twenty industrial families control about 66 per cent of the total industrial-assets, about 79 per cent of the insurance funds and about 80 per cent of the total assets of the banking system'.[3] Most of the new industry is in West Pakistan.

It is clear that there is great inefficiency[4] in this pampered new industry. The industrial licensing system limits competition and, together with exchange licensing, practically guarantees all firms against bankruptcy. Profits are largely windfalls supplied by bureaucratic patronage. The government introduced anti-monopoly regulations in 1969 designed to avoid interlocking of interest between business and banks. There has also been a drive against corrupt businessmen and officials as there was in 1958, and there is some talk of nationalization. The new minimum wage law is intended to benefit workers at the expense of profits. However, the fundamental nature of the control and licensing system remains unchanged, and the measures so far taken are only temporary palliatives.

There are now 4·5 million workers in industry and construction

[1] See G. F. Papanek, *Pakistan's Development*, Harvard, 1967, pp. 40–6. The entrepreneurs were mainly from former trading communities (quasi-castes) of Memons, Chiniotis, Bohra, Khoja Isnashari and Khoja Ismaeli.

[2] See G. F. Papanek, *op. cit.*, p. 67. It would appear that sales of government enterprise since then have been made to newcomers, particularly in East Pakistan.

[3] M. ul Haq, 'A Critical Review of the Third Five Year Plan', in M. A. Khan (ed.), *Management and National Growth*, West Pakistan Management Association, Karachi, 1968, p. 27. The source of these figures is not clear, but G. F. Papanek, *op. cit.*, pp. 67–72, also suggests that there is an extreme degree of concentration in Pakistan.

[4] See N. Islam, 'Comparative Costs, Factor Proportions and Industrial Efficiency in Pakistan', *Pakistan Development Review*, Summer 1967, for a detailed analysis (which unfortunately excludes the textile industries).

(about 11 per cent of the labour force). In 1950 there were only 1·6 million (6 per cent of the labour force). These workers were recruited partly from farming and partly from rural handicrafts which have suffered competition from the new manufactures. The wages and living standards of industrial workers are higher than those of peasants as they need some incentive to come to the city and they need better health and nutrition to stand the pace of industrial life. They have a better water supply, sewerage, hospitals, education than people in the countryside. They see more movies and smoke more cigarettes. However, the surplus of rural labour and government policy in repressing trade union activity kept real wages constant or even declining until the strikes at the end of the Ayub regime in 1969. Workers received less than a third of industrial value added. They have no social security, no facilities for upgrading and training. Since then, their position has been improved by minimum wage legislation (which applies in establishments with more than fifty workers) and improved rights for trade unions. The minimum wage levels fixed in 1969 involved substantial pay increases for the lowest paid workers and the 50 per cent improvement at the bottom sparked off a series of strikes to preserve the differentials of more skilled workers, and to secure increases in the public service, particularly for school teachers. Some of these strikes provoked retaliatory action by the government, and it is not at all clear whether trade unions will really be able to operate freely.

Regional Disparities in Income

The most difficult political problem in Pakistan is undoubtedly the regional disparity between the income levels in East and West. *Per capita* income in the East is only two-thirds of that in the West in money terms, and in real terms is less because Eastern prices are higher. The East is much less urbanized than the West, has many more people in agriculture, and all economic indicators show it to be worse off than the West. There has also been a serious discrepancy in growth rates which has accentuated the income differential. During the Third Plan the average rate of investment in East Pakistan was only 10 per cent of its G.D.P. compared with 20 per cent in the West. In East Pakistan *per capita* consumption is about the same as it was at independence. The East Pakistan economy has also been more unstable than that in the West.

There are several reasons why there was stagnation in the East. The capital city was located (and then expensively re-located) in the West, and a majority of the bureaucrats are concentrated there. The army is largely recruited in the West, and the bulk of it is stationed there.

Over three-quarters of current government expenditure is disbursed in West Pakistan. We can add to this almost 100 per cent of the spending of 2,000 relatively wealthy foreign diplomats and their families. This built up the market for industrial products in the West and provided capital for private investment. As a result, less than a quarter of private investment took place in East Pakistan. In fact, these important reasons for regional disparity are seldom mentioned, whereas there is fierce argument about regional allocation of 'plan' expenditure.

As far as 'development' expenditure of government is concerned, East Pakistan also got much less than its fair share, though the central government tried to disguise this, by treating expenditure on irrigation on the Indus as 'non-plan' investment. West Pakistan got all the benefit from the large 'non-plan' investment in the Indus Basin Works. In the Second Plan this amounted to Rs. 2,910 million and in the third about Rs. 4,000 million. The Indus Works were designed to replace the water supply which was claimed by India.[1] For this reason, the central government authorities always argued that expenditure on the Indus Works provided no net benefit to West Pakistan, but simply compensated for a politically determined loss of water supply. In fact, the Indus Works were not simply a replacement operation: (a) they provided some extra water (as India did not divert all the water until after the works were finished); (b) by feeding the canals from a reservoir rather than a river, the water flow became more dependable and hence more useful because its delivery could be matched to the time pattern of crop requirements. The very large seasonal and annual fluctuations were reduced; (c) the Indus Works provided a good deal of electricity. Furthermore, there was a large amount of irrigation investment in West Pakistan in addition to the Indus Basin Works, so that irrigation water has increased by three-quarters since 1947. The policy of concentrating

[1] The Indus Waters Treaty of 1960 gave Pakistan full water rights to the Indus, the Jhelum and Chenab rivers, and gave India the right to divert all flows of the Ravi, Beas and Sutlej for her own use after a ten-year transitional period ending in 1970. In order to substitute for the waters of the Eastern rivers, a series of large link canals would transfer water from the Indus, Jhelum and Chenab to canals previously watered from the Ravi, Beas and Sutlej. The rivers diverted by India had an annual average discharge in West Pakistan of 25 million acre feet. The other rivers provided 142 M.A.F.; thus West Pakistan would lose 15 per cent of her normal supply of river water ('effective' rainfall is only 10 M.A.F.). This was to be financed by the Indus Basin Development Fund of $895 million (including $174 million provided by India). This was supposed to cover both foreign and domestic costs (though some of the funds were loans not gifts). In fact, the costs will be more than twice this. In 1963 the World Bank raised another $315 million for Pakistan for these works.

Table VII-3

Regional Pattern of Public Expenditure and of Private Investment in Pakistan 1950–70

(Rs. million at current prices)

	1950–55	1955–60	1960–65	1965–70
Current expenditure of Government				
East Pakistan	1,710	2,540	4,340	6,480
West Pakistan	7,200	8,980	12,840	22,230
Development expenditure of Government				
East Pakistan	700	1,970	6,700	11,060
West Pakistan	2,000	4,640	10,010	13,700
Private development expenditure				
East Pakistan	300	730	3,000	5,500
West Pakistan	2,000	2,930	10,700	16,000

Source: Reports of the Advisory Panels for the Fourth Five Year Plan, 1970–5, Planning Commission, Islamabad, 1970.

investment disproportionately on West Pakistan was encouraged by foreign aid donors. A large part of the Indus Basin work was financed by foreign aid, which was motivated by the idea of preventing conflict between India and Pakistan and would probably not have been available for other purposes.

The replacement phase of the Indus Works was completed in 1967 with the Mangla dam on the Jhelum. The second phase was the building of a huge dam on the Indus at Tarbela. This was clearly of a different character as it was an addition to the water supply of West Pakistan. It also happens to be the world's biggest development project. It will take 7·5 years to construct. Its total cost, including power generation, was estimated at $1,047 million, of which $554 million was in foreign exchange. Furthermore, the dam will silt up in fifty years, and its proper exploitation will require other massive investments. Tarbela was justified as part of the Indus Basin Works (rather than as part of normal West Pakistan irrigation expenditure, which is also large) on the ground that the extra water would compensate for the increased cost of maintaining the new replacement irrigation in the West. This was a rather thin argument, but it did succeed in getting foreign aid which might not otherwise have been available. If the foreign aid available for Tarbela had been equally available for other projects, its construction could not have been justified at that point of time.

The main objection to Tarbela is its immense size and delayed impact. It concentrates massive resources of foreign exchange on a project which will not yield benefits until 1975. It now appears that the burden of Tarbela will be so big that it will be difficult to finance supporting investment in tubewell drainage which is necessary to use Tarbela's water beneficially. If the drainage works are not carried out the Tarbela water 'can spell disaster by aggravating water logging which in turn will accentuate salinity and alkalinity'. Because of cost escalations and a reduction in aid, half the cost of Tarbela was being met by Pakistan during the Third Plan, which is a much bigger ratio than for the Indus Works of the Second Plan. Tarbela is a gigantic millstone round the neck of Pakistani planners which prevents any flexibility in resource allocation.

East Pakistan has paid for a good deal of West Pakistan development via the foreign exchange system. Because of the overvalued currency, East Pakistan has received low prices for its raw material exports and has paid high prices for manufactured imports from West Pakistan. Estimates of the balance of trade and invisibles of East and West Pakistan at 'scarcity prices', i.e. valuing the rupee at a realistic shadow exchange rate, show East Pakistan with a deficit of Rs. 4 billion from 1948 to 1968, whereas West Pakistan had a Rs. 55 billion deficit. This means that virtually all the net benefits of foreign aid went to West Pakistan.[1] There has been a substantial drain from East to West, and East Pakistan has been treated as if it were a colony of the West.

There were, of course, some other facts which affected regional performance. There was more entrepreneurial ability in the West, a higher initial income level and better infrastructure. The cropped area is 60 per cent bigger in West Pakistan than in the East. There has been quicker progress in developing new varieties of wheat in the West than new varieties of rice suitable for monsoon conditions. This was due in large part to the longer research on wheat (in Mexico) than on rice (in the Philippines), but may have been influenced by the greater poverty of farmers in the East. Finally, a great deal more research had been done on the possibilities for large-scale irrigation in the West than on the flood control and irrigation potential in the East.

The disparities in income and in economic growth between East and West Pakistan are probably no greater than those between some of the states in India, but they have had greater political significance in Pakistan, because a large part of the differential was demonstrably

[1] See Planning Commission, *Reports of the Advisory Panels for the Five Year Plan 1970-75*, Vol. I, Islamabad, 1970, p. 80.

due to the policies of a strong central government which could have followed different options. More government current expenditure could have been channelled to East Pakistan by locating government offices there, recruiting more of the army there, or even locating the capital there. The exchange rate mechanism could have been made to work in a way fairer to East Pakistan, and a greater proportion of development spending could have been located there.

After the tragic events of March 1971, it is even more difficult to see any prospects for growth in East Pakistan. West Pakistan's capacity to transfer resources to the East is limited, the prospects for foreign aid are bleak, and a good part of East Pakistan's intelligentsia has been destroyed or is in exile. On the whole, therefore, we must conclude that Pakistan's policy of putting growth before equity has proved catastrophic.

Appendix A
Population

Table A-1

Population of Undivided India (Including Native States) Benchmark and Census Years 1600–1941

(millions)

	Undivided India	Native States	British India
1600	125·0		
1700	153·0		
1800	186·0		
1856	227·0		
1871	255·2		
1881	257·4		
1891	282·1		
1901	285·3	62·3	222·2
1911	303·0	71·0	232·1
1921	305·7	72·0	233·7
1931	338·2	82·0	256·2
1941	389·0	93·0	296·0

Source: K. Davis, *The Population of India and Pakistan*, Princeton, N.J., 1951, pp. 26–7. Burma is excluded throughout. The figures for 1931 and 1941 are from the census; 1871–1921 include Davis's adjustment for undercoverage. The figure for 1600 is Davis's adjustment of Moreland's figure. The figure for 1856 is from M. Mukherjee, *National Income of India*, Statistical Publishing Society, Calcutta, 1969. Figures for 1700 and 1800 are my own interpolation of 1600 and 1856. I assume that before 1800 the British conquest made little significant difference to population trends and that the growth path for 1600 to 1800 was smooth at 0·2 per cent a year, and from 1800 to 1856 0·4 per cent. Proportions in British India and Indian States from S. Sivasubramonian, *op. cit.*

Table A-2

Population of Undivided India (Including Native States) 1900–46

(millions on October 1st)

1900	284·5	1925	319·9
1901	286·2	1926	323·2
1902	288·0	1927	326·4
1903	289·7	1928	329·7
1904	291·5	1929	333·1
1905	293·3	1930	336·4
1906	295·1	1931	341·0
1907	296·9	1932	345·8
1908	298·7	1933	350·7
1909	300·5	1934	355·6
1910	302·1	1935	360·6
1911	303·1	1936	365·7
1912	303·4	1937	370·9
1913	303·7	1938	376·1
1914	304·0	1939	381·4
1915	304·2	1940	386·8
1916	304·5	1941	391·7
1917	304·8	1942	396·3
1918	305·1	1943	400·3
1919	305·3	1944	405·6
1920	305·6	1945	410·4
1921	307·3	1946	415·2
1922	310·4		
1923	313·6		
1924	316·7		

Source: S. Sivasubramonian, *op. cit.*

Appendix B

Real National Income by Industrial Origin

The most thorough published study of Indian national income is the recent volume by M. Mukherjee, *National Income of India*, Statistical Publishing Society, Calcutta, 1969, who reviews most previous estimates as well as presenting some of his own (p. 61). However, his estimates are derived by linking estimates of other people at different points of time or averaging different series of other estimators. It is thus a very eclectic bundle of numbers, and no breakdown is available by sector. Furthermore, his finding that real income per head rose appreciably in the last half century of British rule is inconsistent with Blyn's painstaking estimates of agricultural production which show a fall in farm output per head. Detailed estimates of real national income by sector of the economy have been made by S. Sivasubramonian, which are as yet unpublished. These also show a rise in total output per head, but a fall in agricultural output per head.

I have, therefore, made my own crude estimates of real national income by sector which remove this inconsistency. I have relied almost entirely on the work of Blyn and Sivasubramonian, but with substantial adjustments.

For the agricultural sector, crop output was estimated by using the 'modified all crop' yield figures (for British India) of G. Blyn, *Agricultural Trends in India, 1891–1947*, University of Pennsylvania, 1966, pp. 349–50, by the area estimates (for Undivided India) of S. Sivasubramonian, *National Income of India 1900–1901 to 1946–47* (mimeographed), Delhi School of Economics, Delhi, 1965. Blyn's figures at 1924–8 prices are adjusted to 1938 prices by using Sivasubramonian's implicit price ratios, and Blyn's figures are also adjusted upwards by 59·36 per cent as they refer to only eighteen crops. The ratio of output of eighteen crops to total crops was taken from 1960 data given in the Central Statistical Organization, *Brochure on Revised Series of National Product for 1960–61 to 1964–65*, Delhi, August 1967, which gives figures for sixty-eight crops. The inputs were deducted by using Sivasubramonian's ratio for 1938.

Output in the factory sector of manufacturing was taken from Sivasubramonian. Output of small-scale industry was assumed to move parallel with employment. Output of transport, trade and communication was assumed to move parallel to material product (i.e. agriculture plus industry), housing services to move parallel to population, and output in other sectors to move parallel to employment in the sector concerned.

Table B-1

Net Domestic Product of Undivided India (Including Native States) by Industrial Origin at 1938 Factor Cost

(Rs. billion in fiscal years)

Year	Agriculture, Forestry and Fishing	Mining, Manufacturing and Small Enterprises	Other	Net Domestic Product
1900	13·1	2·7	6·9	22·7
1901	12·9	2·8	7·0	22·8
1902	14·5	2·9	7·2	24·7
1903	14·4	2·9	7·2	24·5
1904	13·5	2·9	7·1	23·5
1905	13·9	3·0	7·2	24·1
1906	14·6	3·0	7·4	25·0
1907	12·6	3·0	7·1	22·6
1908	14·0	3·0	7·3	24·2
1909	16·3	3·0	7·6	26·9
1910	16·3	3·0	7·7	26·9
1911	15·6	3·0	7·6	26·1
1912	15·9	3·0	7·6	26·6
1913	15·1	3·0	7·5	25·6
1914	16·1	3·0	7·7	26·7
1915	16·3	3·0	7·8	27·1
1916	17·9	3·0	8·3	29·2
1917	16·9	2·9	8·3	28·1
1918	12·9	2·8	7·7	23·5
1919	16·6	2·8	8·0	27·5
1920	13·9	2·8	7·4	24·1
1921	16·2	2·8	7·7	26·7
1922	16·5	2·8	7·8	27·1
1923	15·9	2·7	7·6	26·3
1924	15·9	2·9	7·7	26·5
1925	16·0	2·9	7·7	26·6
1926	16·4	3·0	7·9	27·3
1927	15·9	3·1	7·9	26·9
1928	16·7	2·9	8·0	27·6
1929	17·0	3·1	8·1	28·2
1930	17·2	2·9	8·1	28·2
1931	16·8	2·9	8·0	27·7
1932	17·2	2·9	8·1	28·1
1933	17·8	2·9	8·2	28·8
1934	17·1	3·1	8·2	28·4
1935	17·1	3·3	8·2	28·6
1936	18·1	3·4	8·4	30·0
1937	17·9	3·7	8·5	30·0

Table B-1 (*contd*)

Year	Agriculture, Forestry and Fishing	Mining, Manufacturing and Small Enterprises	Other	Net Domestic Product
1938	16·4	4·0	8·3	28·7
1939	17·7	4·1	8·7	30·4
1940	17·8	4·2	8·8	30·7
1941	17·1	4·5	8·9	30·6
1942	17·8	4·7	9·5	32·0
1943	19·2	4·9	10·2	34·3
1944	18·5	4·8	10·4	33·7
1945	17·9	5·0	10·5	33·4
1946	18·0	4·5	10·0	32·5

Table B-2

'Conventional' Estimates of Net Domestic Product of
India by Industrial Origin at 1948 Factor Cost

(Rs. billion in fiscal years)

Year	Agriculture, Forestry and Fishing	Mining, Manufacturing and Small Enterprises	Other	Net Domestic Product
1946	(42·4)	(14·7)	(32·6)	(89·7)
1947	(45·9)	(15·1)	(30·4)	(91·4)
1948	42·5	14·8	29·4	86·7
1949	43·6	14·6	30·2	88·4
1950	43·4	14·8	30·5	88·7
1951	44·4	15·2	31·6	91·2
1952	46·0	15·8	32·9	94·7
1953	49·8	16·5	34·0	100·3
1954	50·3	17·0	35·5	102·8
1955	50·2	17·6	37·0	104·8
1956	52·5	18·4	39·0	109·9
1957	50·1	18·6	40·3	109·0
1958	55·6	18·8	42·3	116·7
1959	55·1	19·7	44·1	118·9
1960	59·0	21·1	47·7	127·8
1961	59·1	22·2	50·1	131·3
1962	57·9	23·0	53·0	133·9
1963	59·7	24·4	56·5	140·6
1964	65·1	25·3	60·7	151·1
1965	57·2	26·6	64·0	147·8
1966	57·3	27·2	66·7	151·2
1967				
1968				
1969				

Source: Rough estimates for 1946–8 from M. Mukherjee, *op. cit.*, p. 130, deflated by the price index on p. 94. 1948–60 from Central Statistical Organization, *Estimates of National Income 1948–49 to 1962–63*, Delhi, February 1964; 1960–6 from Central Statistical Organization, *Estimates of National Product 1960–61 to 1966–67*, Delhi, October 1967. According to a cryptic note on p. 24 of the national income publication issued in 1963, it would appear that the figures for 1960 and subsequent years are overstated by 1·1 per cent, because of an increase in coverage of agricultural statistics. It is not clear why the Central Statistical Organization has not made an appropriate correction.

169

Table B-3

Net Domestic Product of Pakistan by Industrial Origin at 1959 Factor Cost

(Rs. billion in fiscal years)

Year	Agriculture, Forestry and Fishing	Mining, Manufacturing and Small Enterprises	Other	Net Domestic Product
1947				
1948	(14·2)	(1·3)		
1949	13·9	1·4	7·8	23·0
1950	14·4	1·5	8·0	23·8
1951	13·8	1·6	8·4	23·8
1952	14·2	1·7	8·6	24·5
1953	15·2	1·9	8·9	26·1
1954	14·9	2·1	9·1	26·1
1955	14·4	2·3	9·4	26·0
1956	15·5	2·4	9·7	27·6
1957	15·3	2·5	9·9	27·8
1958	15·1	2·7	10·3	28·1
1959	15·9	2·8	10·7	29·4
1960	16·4	3·1	11·3	30·8
1961	17·3	3·4	12·0	32·7
1962	17·4	3·7	12·8	33·9
1963	18·4	4·1	14·2	36·8
1964	18·8	4·4	15·1	38·3
1965	19·1	4·7	16·3	40·0
1966	19·3	5·0	17·7	41·2
1967	21·4	5·3	18·5	45·2
1968	22·0	5·6	19·9	47·6
1969				

Source: 1949–65 from *Twenty Years of Pakistan in Statistics 1947–1967*, C.S.O., Karachi, 1968; 1966–8 from *Monthly Statistical Bulletin*, C.S.O., Karachi, January 1970. 1948 figures are my own rough estimates based on indicators in the first cited document.

Table B-4

Gross National Product and Gross Regional Product
of Pakistan at 1959 Factor Cost

(Rs. million in fiscal years)

Fiscal Year	Pakistan	East Pakistan	West Pakistan
1948	(25,828)	(13,369)	(12,459)
1949	24,962	12,352	12,610
1950	26,536	13,072	13,464
1951	26,275	13,254	13,021
1952	26,725	13,647	13,078
1953	28,168	13,841	14,327
1954	28,760	14,109	14,651
1955	28,346	13,355	14,991
1956	30,205	14,772	15,433
1957	30,562	14,463	16,099
1958	30,505	14,175	16,330
1959	31,439	14,934	16,505
1960	33,086	15,775	17,311
1961	35,043	16,681	18,362
1962	36,284	16,591	19,693
1963	39,284	18,352	20,932
1964	41,058	18,544	22,514
1965	42,968	19,446	23,522
1966	45,133	19,697	25,436
1967	48,536	21,321	27,215
1968	51,449	22,189	29,260
1969	54,276	23,119	31,157

Source: 1949–69 from *Reports of the Advisory Panels
for the Fourth Five Year Plan, 1970–75*,
Islamabad, May 1970. 1948 is my estimate
based on movement in agricultural output
between 1948 and 1949 as given in *Twenty
Years of Pakistan in Statistics*, C.S.O.,
Karachi, 1968.

Table B-5

Total Cropped Area* in Undivided India (Including Native States), India and Pakistan 1900–70

(million acres in fiscal years)

Year	Undivided India	Year	Undivided India	Year	India	Pakistan
1900	271·6	1924	311·8	1947		54·0
1901	266·5	1925	307·6	1948	276·5	56·2
1902	276·2	1926	306·8	1949	321·2	n.a.
1903	284·1	1927	307·1	1950	325·9	58·1
1904	283·9	1928	315·9	1951		57·0
1905	278·3	1929	311·9	1952		57·4
1906	296·4	1930	318·3	1953		60·6
1907	283·6	1931	320·9	1954		60·3
1908	299·0	1932	317·3	1955	364·0	60·3
1909	306·4	1933	324·4	1956	369·4	60·9
1910	309·2	1934	313·4	1957	360·3	60·3
1911	298·6	1935	316·2	1958	374·6	61·1
1912	306·1	1936	324·1	1959	377·6	61·9
1913	296·2	1937	322·3	1960	377·3	62·1
1914	313·7	1938	318·2	1961	385·7	63·9
1915	301·9	1939	318·5	1962	387·5	64·6
1916	317·5	1940	328·2	1963	387·5	64·9
1917	320·5	1941	320·6	1964	390·7	68·7
1918	267·7	1942	331·1	1965	383·7	68·8
1919	303·8	1943	337·6	1966	387·0	
1920	280·5	1944	346·5	1967		
1921	304·4	1945	338·7	1968		
1922	308·9	1946	334·0	1969		
1923	305·2			1970		

* Cropped area includes all sown land (counted twice if sown twice).

Source: Undivided India from S. Sivasubramonian, *op. cit.;* Pakistan 1947–65 from *Twenty Years of Pakistan in Statistics 1947–67*, C.S.O., Karachi, 1968, p. 36. India 1948–50 and 1955–66 from *Pocketbook of Economic Information 1969*, Ministry of Finance, Delhi, p. 43.

Select Bibliography

BOOKS

Abul Fazl, *Ain i Akbari of Abul Fazl-I-Allami*, Vol. II, H. S. Jarrett and J. Sarkar (eds), Calcutta, 1949.

M. A. Ali, *The Moghul Nobility Under Aurangzeb*, Asia Publishing House, London, 1966.

F. Anstey, *The Economic Development of India*, Longmans Green, London, 1929.

S. Avineri (ed.), *Karl Marx on Colonialism and Modernization*, Doubleday, New York, 1969.

F. G. Bailey, *Caste and the Economic Frontier*, Manchester University Press, 1957.

F. Bernier, *Travels in the Moghul Empire 1956–68*, revised edition by A. Constable, London, 1891.

A. Beteille, *Caste, Class, and Power*, Cambridge University Press, 1966.

A. Beteille, *Castes Old and New*, Asia Publishing House, Bombay, 1969.

G. Blyn, *Agricultural Trends in India, 1891–1947*, Oxford University Press, London, 1966.

H. Bolitho, *Jinnah: Creator of Pakistan*, Murray, London, 1964.

D. H. Buchanan, *The Development of Capitalistic Enterprise in India*, F. Cass, London, 1966.

K. Davis, *The Population of India and Pakistan*, Princeton University Press, 1951.

R. C. Desai, *Standard of Living in India and Pakistan 1931–32 to 1940–41*, Popular Book Depot, Bombay, 1953.

P. N. Dhar and A. F. Lydall, *The Role of Small Enterprise in Indian Manufacturing*, Asia Publishing House, Bombay, 1961.

R. C. Dutt, *The Economic History of India*, 2 vols, Routledge, London, 1963.

R. P. Dutt, *India Today*, Gollancz, London, 1940.

M. Edwardes, *British India 1772–1947*, Sidgwick and Jackson, London, 1967.

R. E. Frykenberg, *Land Control and Social Structure in Indian History*, Madison, 1969.

D. R. Gadgil, *The Industrial Evolution of India in Recent Times*, 4th edition, Oxford University Press, Calcutta, 1942.

M. K. Gandhi, *The Story of My Experiments with Truth*, Navajivan, Ahmedabad, 1948.

B. N. Ganguli (ed.), *Readings in Indian Economic History*, Asia Publishing House, London, 1964.

S. Ghose, *The Renaissance to Militant Nationalism in India*, Allied Publishers, Bombay, 1969.

I. M. Habib, *Agrarian System of Moghul India (1556–1707)*, Asia Publishing House, London, 1963.

M. ul Haq, *The Strategy of Economic Planning*, Oxford University Press, London, 1966.

W. W. Hunter, *The Indian Mussalmans*, Premier Book House, Lahore, 1964 (reprint of 1871 edition).

N. Kaldor, *Indian Tax Reform*, Ministry of Planning, New Delhi, 1956.

M. Ayub Khan, *Friends Not Masters*, Oxford University Press, Lahore, 1967.

D. Kumar, *Land and Caste in South India*, Cambridge University Press, 1965.

A. I. Levkovsky, *Capitalism in India*, People's Publishing House, Bombay, 1966.

O. Lewis, *Village Life in Northern India*, Random House, New York, 1958.

B. B. Misra, *The Indian Middle Classes*, Oxford University Press, 1961.

W. H. Moreland, *The Agrarian System of Moslem India*, Cambridge, 1929.

W. H. Moreland, *India at the Death of Akbar*, A. Ram, Delhi, 1962.

W. H. Moreland, *India from Akbar to Aurangzeb*, Macmillan, London, 1923.

W. H. Moreland and P. Geyl, *Jahangir's India*, Heffer, Cambridge, 1925.

M. Mukherjee, *National Income of India*, Statistical Publishing Society, Calcutta, 1969.

E. M. S. Namboodiripad, *Economics and Politics of India's Socialist Pattern*, Peoples Publishing House, Delhi, 1966.

D. Naoroji, *Poverty and Un-British Rule in India*, London, 1901.

P. Nath, *A Study in the Economic Condition of Ancient India*, Royal Asiatic Society, London, 1929.

W. C. Neale, *Economic Change in Rural India*, Yale University Press, 1962.

J. Nehru, *The Discovery of India*, Asia Publishing House, London, 1965.

J. Nehru, *Glimpses of World History*, Lindsay Drummond, London, 1945.

J. Nehru, *Toward Freedom: The Autobiography of Jawarharlal Nehru*, Day, New York, 1941.

G. F. Papanek, *Pakistan's Development: Social Goals and Private Incentives*, Oxford University Press, 1968.

I. H. Qureshi, *History of the Muslim Community in India*, Mouton, The Hague, 1962.

P. N. Rosenstein-Rodan (ed.), *Pricing and Fiscal Policies*, Allen and Unwin, London, 1964.

K. B. Sayeed, *Pakistan, The Formative Phase*, Oxford University Press, 1968.

K. B. Sayeed, *The Political System of Pakistan*, Allen and Unwin, London, 1968.

S. Sivasubramonian, *National Income of India 1900–1 to 1946–7*, Delhi School of Economics, 1965 (mimeographed).

D. E. Smith, *India as a Secular State*, Princeton University Press, 1963.

M. N. Srinivas, *Caste in Modern India*, Asia Publishing House, Bombay, 1962.

M. N. Srinivas (ed.), *India's Villages*, Asia Publishing House, Bombay, 1969.

M. N. Srinivas, *Social Change in Modern India*, Cambridge University Press, 1966.

E. Stokes, *The English Utilitarians and India*, Oxford, 1959.

P. Streeten and M. Lipton, *The Crisis of Indian Planning*, Oxford University Press, London, 1968.

D. Thorner, *The Agrarian Prospect in India*, Delhi School of Economics, 1956.

D. and A. Thorner, *Land and Labour in India*, Asia Publishing House, New York, 1962.

M. Weber, *The Religion of India*, Collier-Macmillan, 1967.

P. Woodruff, *The Men who Ruled India*, Vol. I, 1953, Vol. II, 1954, Cape, London.

ARTICLES

A. Maddison, 'The Historical Origins of Indian Poverty,' *Banca Nazionale del Lavoro Quarterly Review*, March 1970.

M. D. Morris, 'Economic Change and Agriculture in Nineteenth Century India', *Indian Economic and Social History Review*, June 1966.

M. D. Morris, 'Towards a Reinterpretation of Nineteenth Century Indian Economic History', *The Journal of Economic History*, December 1963.

M. D. Morris, 'Trends and Tendencies in Indian History', *Indian Economic and Social History Review*, December 1968.

M. D. Morris and B. Stein, 'The Economic History of India: A Bibliographic Essay', *The Journal of Economic History*, June 1961.

T. Raychaudhuri, 'A Reinterpretation of Nineteenth Century Indian Economic History', *Indian Economic and Social History Review*, March 1968.

M. J. T. Thavaraj, 'Rate of Public Investment in India, 1898–1938', *Contributions to Indian Economic History II*, edited by T. Raychaudhuri, Mukhopadhyay, Calcutta, 1963.

OFFICIAL PUBLICATIONS

Government of India

Administrative Reforms Commission, *District Administration*, Delhi, February 1967.

Administrative Reforms Commission, *Public Sector Undertakings*, Delhi, 1969.

Central Statistical Organization, *Brochure on Revised Series of National Product for 1960–61 to 1964–65*, Delhi, August 1967.

Education Commission, *Report on Education and National Development*, New Delhi, 1966.

175

Ministry of Finance, *Economic Survey 1969–70*, Delhi, 1970.

Planning Commission, *The First Five Year Plan*, Delhi, 1952.

Planning Commission, *Papers Relating to the Formulation of the Second Five Year Plan*, Delhi, 1955.

Planning Commission, *Second Five Year Plan*, Delhi, 1956.

Planning Commission, *Third Five Year Plan*, Delhi, 1961.

Planning Commission, *Fourth Five Year Plan, A Draft Outline*, Delhi, 1966.

Planning Commission, *Fourth Five Year Plan 1969–1974*, Delhi, 1970.

Planning Commission, *Implementation of Land Reforms*, Delhi, 1966.

Planning Commission, *Report of the Committee on Distribution of Income and Levels of Living*, Part I, Delhi, 1964, Part II, Delhi, 1969.

Government of Kerala

State Planning Board, *Alternate Policies for the Fourth Five Year Plan*, Kerala, 1969.

Government of Pakistan

Central Statistical Office, *Twenty Years of Pakistan in Statistics 1947–1967*, Karachi, 1968.

Ministry of Finance, *The Budget in Brief (Final)*, Islamabad, 1970.

Ministry of Health, Labour and Family Planning, *Labour Policy of Government of Pakistan*, Islamabad, 1969.

National Planning Board, *The First Five Year Plan 1955–60*, Karachi, 1957.

Planning Commission, *The Second Five Year Plan 1960–65*, Karachi, 1960.

Planning Commission, *Final Evaluation of the Second Five Year Plan 1960–65*, Karachi, 1966.

Planning Commission, *The Third Five Year Plan 1965–70*, Karachi, 1965.

Planning Commission, *Socio-Economic Objectives of the Fourth Five Year Plan 1970–75*, Islamabad, 1968.

Planning Commission, *The Fourth Five Year Plan 1970–75*, Islamabad, 1970.

Planning Commission, *Reports of the Advisory Panels for the Fourth Five Year Plan 1970–75*, Islamabad, 1970.

Report of the Pay and Services Commission 1959–62, Islamabad, 1969.

Index

179